Magick Works

STORIES OF OCCULTISM IN THEORY AND PRACTICE

Julian Vayne

Also available
Now That's What I Call Chaos Magick (with Greg Humphries)
Pharmakon

Contents

Thank you

To my friends and family, to those ancestors who dared to explore the shadows of delicious possibility.

To my teachers, animal, vegetable and mineral. Thank you all those people who have contributed to the wealth of material that comprises the internet. Special thanks to Alec, Amba & The Divine Soror Res for proofing and valuable comments.

Thanks to the Brighton PACT group, the Order of Bards, Ovates and Druids, the Illuminates of Thanateros and The Coven of the Silver Wheel. Thank you White Goddess for helping me enter the desert of the Abyss and to Mother Yemaja for pulling me out.

My work is the confluence of ideas, many of which flow from other people. I would especially like to thank my partner Helen for her invaluable advice, comments and love.

Contact

The Magical Pact of The Illuminates of Thanateros (IOT)

Applications for membership should be made in writing to:

Novice Guide
BM8482
London
WC1N 3XX

for background information
http://www.iot.org.uk/

The Order of Bards, Ovates and Druids (OBOD)

PO Box 1333, Lewes, East Sussex BN7 1DX, England
http://www.druidry.org/

Introduction

Some of the texts that follow are taken from academic lectures, some from magazine articles and some from workshops. A few of the texts here are essays I've written which have never been published until this volume. Others are transcriptions of rituals, some fleshing out ceremonial instructions with a graphic narrative, while some remaining as the bare instructions provided to participants.

When I came to consider the follow up to the runaway success of *Now That's What I Call Chaos Magick* (which I penned with Greg Humphries in 2004) I'd kicked around various ideas; maybe something focusing on the Qabalah? Perhaps a book that looked at the relationship of witchcraft and the modern occult tradition called 'Chaos Magick'?. With a whole hodgepodge of ideas whirling round my mind I'd gone over to see Peter, a fellow magician who lived just a few streets away from me when I was resident in Brighton.

"I know the kind of things I want to say, what I want to write", I explained, "it's just that I need to find the vehicle, the vessel to pour the ideas into". Peter, an experienced journalist, listened patiently. "Why not just write about your own experiences, write autobiographically," he suggested.

So here it is, a selection of my personal experiences, insights and challenges woven throughout with the golden thread of magick. My hope is that the range of styles in these essays mirrors the diversity and range of approaches that characterise the particular approach to magick that I employ, namely chaos magick. However this book isn't really about me, it's about you. Chances are that as you're reading this then you, like me, have fallen in love with magick. You are burning with the desire to delve into the shadows of the occult. For those of you who are new to the path of magick I trust that you will find these stories and essays of mine useful signposts in your own learning. Of course your story is, and will be, different from mine, your conclusions and opinions may be very different from those I present here. I'm certainly not asking you to follow in my footsteps, for we must all choose and walk a unique path (which I think is one of the key principles if we are to make our magick really powerful). My story is not a star to guide you but rather a lamp that may help illuminate your own way.

For those readers who are experienced sorcerers, I wish is that that my writing may suggest some fresh techniques, but mostly that it will provide a wider context into which you might set your own work. What excites me is the idea that the last 50 or so years have seen the development of an amazing global esoteric community. While the usual bickering between orders and groups still goes on, I think there is something of magickal perestroika in the air. In some small way the writing contained in this volume is proof of this. Here you will read lectures and articles I've been asked to produce for a wide variety of occult and pagan (and indeed academic) audiences. Today it seems to me that people move more easily between many different worlds, engaging with different systems, approaches and beliefs often with a healthy blend of respect, interest and integrity. Certainly I feel honoured that I have been asked to address members of such a range of different esoteric paths. I am also pleased to say that in many of the rituals given here we performed with colleagues from a wide variety of magickal backgrounds; sometimes participants were member of formalised Orders, sometimes not. We should see the boundaries of our orders, cults, covens and groves for what they are, permeable borders. The magick of our Way is not in the insularity of our chosen path but in how it can blend and develop with those other paths around us.

As ever, magick is at the edges, in the liminal space; and the liminal space is not mine or yours, it is above all, a shared reality. I hope you enjoy me sharing these ideas with you.

JSV Devon 2007

What is Magick?

The question 'what is magick?' is at once both the simplest and most complex question that we can ask in the field of occultism. Occultism is of course literally the study of that which is hidden, and magick (whether you prefer to spell it with or without a final 'k') is the hidden power that changes things. Magick is hidden, in part, because it is not generally understood. Arthur C. Clarke asserted "any sufficiently advanced technology is indistinguishable from magic". For example, a person from the 15th century might well describe the flight of a jumbo jet as magickal because its mechanism was beyond their knowledge. However, the term magick suggests much more than simply unknown or misunderstood power; it also refers to the mysterious processes in the universe that underlie all (apparently) understood phenomena and particularly to the ability to influence those processes.

For example; flip a coin and it has a (roughly) fifty-fifty chance of coming down either heads or tails. We know that the metal coin can spin in a variety of complicated ways as it falls through the air, and so whether it will be heads or tails is hard to predict. However, we might take someone who is known to be psychic to a laboratory and successfully demonstrate that they are able to slightly (statistically) influence the fall of the coins, perhaps causing it to fall more times heads uppermost than chance would normally suggest. This kind of psychic ability has been demonstrated time and again in parapsychological laboratories all over the world. There is a small but significant and repeatable (though often elusive) effect - go and read some of the (generally rather dull) experiments if you don't believe me - yes, people are psychic. So that's magick? Making coins fall the way up you want? Well, yes and no! Yes, this kind of effect is part of what magick is but no, that's not the whole story.

Think about it.

There is a coin - the coin is made of atoms. Atoms are not little specks of unbreakable dust like so many tiny billiard balls; instead they are much more ghostly, whirling fields of energy, or probability and change. The truth is that quantum physics demonstrates quite clearly the fact that subatomic particles can wink in and out of existence, travel faster than light, time-travel and react directly to human consciousness. So our apparently 'solid' coin which is being acted upon by the 'mysterious' magickal power of the psychic is in reality no less ghostly than the paranormal power of making the coin fall heads, heads, heads, heads…

And what else about our coin? Well what is a coin? A symbol, it is a promise, a token, designed and acted upon by the human imagination in such a way that I can exchange this fairly useless disk of metal for something much more useful (such as an apple, or exchanging many such disks - a copy of this book!). The coin is a product of the human imagination. Look around you. Every manufactured object around you existed first in the human imagination, in that ghostly, hidden, occult realm within our heads. And of course let's not forget that your imagination exists because of your brain, and your brain exists because of atoms and atoms are these fuzzy zones of probability and possibility. Whilst I do agree that coins tend to stay as coins, it's worth considering that there is no reason (in terms of the subatomic physics of the thing) that coins don't turn into beautiful flowers or automobiles or black holes!

So what has this got to do with magick?

I believe that magick is the thing that holds the universe together. It is magick that is responsible for the fact that coins tend to stay as coins; just as it is magick that is responsible for the way the psychic can influence the ways that it falls. Magick is rather like the eastern concept of the Tao - it is the changing, moving power that underlies all things. We can seek to know magick through witchcraft (of either the Wiccan variety or other forms), shamanism, Qabalistic magick, Tantra or any other system. Each system provides a range of tools to get to grips with what magick is. In my opinion all these different ways of understanding magick are like different styles of painting. Witchcraft, for example, is one style: it comes complete with a preferred set of tools (cords, magick circles, god and goddess images, initiatory systems etc) - Qabalistic magick is another style (tools including ceremonial magick, fasting and prayer, pathworking, vibration of names of power etc). You can choose to become adept at one or more styles and many people explore a whole range as they develop over time. The styles to watch out for are those who say "you can ONLY get to magick (or God or enlightenment or whatever) through this one method" - by all means explore those styles

9

if you like but if you want my advice don't give 'em your credit card details!

Oh yes and don't take any style too seriously.

So what do other writers say in answer to the question 'what is magick?' Well, from a variety of different people (each with their preferred style or styles of occultism) here are a few answers:

> "Magic, the art of sensing, and shaping the subtle, unseen forces that flow through the world, of awakening deeper levels of consciousness beyond the rational, is an element common to all Witchcraft traditions ... "
>
> Starhawk

> "... magic is 'using the power of the mind to nudge probabilities.'"
>
> Janina Renee

> "Magic is a convenient word for a whole collection of techniques, all of which involve the mind. In this case, we might conceive of these techniques as included the mobilization of confidence, will, and emotion brought about by the recognition of necessity; the use of imaginative faculties, particularly the ability to visualize, in order to begin to understand how other beings function in nature so we can use this knowledge to achieve necessary ends."
>
> Margot Adler

> "the arts of exchanging consciousness and energy between differing worlds."
>
> R.J. Stewart

> "Magick is the Science and Art of causing Change to occur in conformity with Will."
>
> Aleister Crowley

> "Magick is the art of causing changes in consciousness in conformity with the Will."
>
> Dion Fortune

"Sorcery: the systematic cultivation of enhanced consciousness or non-ordinary awareness & its deployment in the world of deeds & objects to bring about desired results."

Hakim Bey

"Real magick is not merely an assortment of skills and techniques. It's more like an open minded attitude, a blend of interest and dedication, which allows each honest mage to observe, to learn, to adapt, and to invent unique ways of changing identity and reality from within."

Jan Fries

"Magic is a set of techniques and approaches which can be used to extend the limits of Achievable Reality. Our sense of Achievable Reality is the limitations which we believe bind us into a narrow range of actions and successes - what we believe to be possible for us at any one time. In this context, the purpose of magic is to simultaneously explore those boundaries and attempt to push them back - to widen the 'sphere' of possible action."

Phil Hine

"Magic is the Highest, most Absolute, and most Divine Knowledge of Natural Philosophy, advanced in its works and wonderful operations by a right understanding of the inward and occult virtue of things; so that true Agents being applied to proper Patients, strange and admirable effects will thereby be produced. Whence magicians are profound and diligent searchers into Nature; they, because of their skill, know how to anticipate an effect, the which to the vulgar shall seem to be a miracle."

The Goetia of the Lemegeton of King Solomon.

Why bother with so many different definitions? Well each author is right, each writer is attempting to describe the essentially indescribable. Magick, as well as being all those things you've read about above, is also a feeling, a sense, an atmosphere and most importantly an experience. Defining exactly what magick is, is like trying to capture the wind in a bottle - an entertaining but impossible task! So what do these definitions have in common? They all suggest change - magick isn't so much a thing or a subject in the way that geography is. Instead it is a process, a journey

11

and a way of exploring the way the world works and the way you can move within that world.

Magick is about doing - so without any more delay let us begin our journey and move from theory to practice...

Back, going back in all directions...

I was born the day after Halloween in 1968 in Stevenage, Hertfordshire, and that's where I grew up. My parents are and were kindly people but as a child I always felt different, set apart. Many people (and sometimes members of my own family) thought that I was 'stuck up', or thought myself better than my peers and, in some respects that was true. For as long as I can remember I've been in love with (or been obsessed by, take your pick) magick.

My parents generally tolerated and even at times supported, my interest. I recall as an eleven year old asking to go to the festival of Mind, Body and Spirit in Olympia, London. Dutifully, my Dad (bless him) took me and kept an eye on me as I wandered around the stalls; aura readings and Kirlean photography, dowsing, meditation techniques and exotic health foods. But over and over, there was one stall that I kept being attracted to. Behind it sat a quiet, bearded man with glasses, dressed fairly conventionally (especially when compared to some of the more flamboyant Eastern cults that were in evidence at the festival). On his stall were books - wonderful books. Books that were bound in black leather and bore silver symbols that I didn't recognise. Incense, sweet with the fragrance of what I later would come to know as frankincense, rose in faintly blue clouds beside him. Arranged beside him were figurines of mysterious gods and goddesses, naked women with crowns shaped like the horns of the new moon, strange unearthly tentacled monsters and a figure, half human, half goat, with wings and pentagram on its forehead. I recall drifting past that particular stall again and again, frustrated that I didn't have enough money to buy anything that was on show, fascinated by the paraphernalia of the occult; crystal balls, rolls of vellum parchment for making talismans, bottles of exotically perfumed oils.

As a child I don't really remember when I became interested in magick, but I know it was very early on. I also know that from as long as I can remember what attracted me was witchcraft. The whole mystery and intensity enchanted me - I would spend hours in the library reading and re-reading the few occult books that Stevenage library possessed (this was years before the world-wide web happened...). I even requested books via inter-library loan such as the *Key of Solomon* and the *Goetia*.

AM -

Get up,

Yoga

meditation - silent in lotus posture, focusing on breathing

Breakfast

Reading

Lunch

PM -

Spell study

Meditation - mantra.

Dinner

Recreation

Practice drawing and visualising pentagrams.

Astral projection exercise (before sleep)

Etc.

Of course, I soon ran into problems. I'd kitted out my bedroom for the purpose of magick - my parents had tolerated me removing my bed so that I slept on a mattress on the floor. Under the carpet I had painted a magick circle with a pentagram in the centre. Although the walls were tiled with cork I'd covered them in black crepe paper and began the process of adding magickal signs all over the room in silver paint, symbols for each of the directions. My aim was to be able to do rituals in my bedroom (ideally when the rest of the family were out). Meditation is all very well but it just wasn't very exciting. Aleister Crowley might be the scary black magician (according to some writers) but if all he really had to say was 'concentrate on your breathing young one!' then that really wasn't what I wanted. I wanted incense, I wanted images of the ancient gods (like the ones on the stall at the festival). I wanted black robes and horned headdresses! I wanted mystery, weird stuff and yes - power!

So bits of my timetable got lost - I'd spend rather longer than I meant to in doing 'spell work'. This consisted of copying spells from any books I could lay my hands on into my own 'book of shadows'. My aim was to end up with a complete Grimoire, a book of magickal techniques. Looking back I'm pleased that I spent so much time doing this. The act of copying out so much information into my own notebooks effectively taught me the association of the four elements, the symbols of the planets used in astrology, the names and meanings of the runes and the Hebrew alphabet. I diligently copied out diagrams of the Qabalah, the Hebrew Tree of Life and the Wiccan wheel of the year.

Of course, outside the world of my temple (my bedroom) life carried on as normal. In fact it was unbearably normal. Stevenage was a 'new town', built after the Second World War. The whole place seemed to me to be dull, boring and pointless. Fortunately I lived on the edge of the town; just a short walk away was the countryside and expanses of wild wasteland that, as I grew up, gradually mutated into more humdrum houses.

I was a small, bespectacled kid. At school I was able to get by through a combination of being clever, playing the fool and making sure that many of my mates were bigger and meaner than me. At home I'd dream about being a superhero (as most children do) 'The Leopard of Lime Street' or 'Triceratops Man'. But, unlike my friends, I thought I might have the means to become a REAL super-man. I'd also discovered that there was a great lie, that characters like 'the devil' were not really evil. Instead they were really images of the horned god, the ancient Pagan god. Satan was really Pan! The blackness of magick was not really about evil, about being mean, but what it was about was power and fear. People, especially those in power (like the Christian priesthood) didn't like the idea of magick because it meant freedom. Of course, it isn't exactly a cut and dried thing. Even within magick there were people who thought the inverted (two points uppermost) pentagram was a symbol of evil, but slowly I came to see how it was really just the sign of the horned god. My instinctive delight when I had seen the horned and hoofed, half human, half goat figure that time at the festival was okay.

I'm really glad the Satanic child abuse thing hadn't hit at that time. On my pencil case I'd drawn a pentagram with horned goat's head within it - below the star read the words 'Drol Natas!' - Lord Satan backwards. Like many people my age (I was ten) I was trying to get a handle on good and evil and trying to understand the complexities of right and wrong. The only difference was that I felt that there was this tremendous power underlying the whole of the universe - an amoral force, like electricity, that you could use to kill or curse, that some people didn't want anyone to tap into.

So although I tried hard to meditate I kept being pulled away towards the more exciting aspects of magick, the paraphernalia, the symbols and the richness of occult symbolism. I learnt it thoroughly but had little practical experience.

I was eleven when circumstances finally conspired to force my hand. I'd been doing yoga for about two years and meditating with little success for about the same length of time. It was nearing Christmas and my family were preparing for the festive season. My dad was anxious to sell his camper van and to use the proceeds of this to fund some of our Christmas cheer. My family had never been wealthy and this year was looking (so I judged from hushed conversations between my parents) like it might be a lean one. I remember my dad sounding exasperated and telling my mum that he didn't think he'd be able to sell the camper at this time of year, or if he did he didn't expect to get anything like the asking price.

It was time, I resolved, to try some practical magick; a spell, which, of course worked.

Cut to a quarter of a century later...

Manifesto of the Magickians

The mind is the first territory, and the imagination is the pervasive element in mind. Magick is the technology of this realm, a system of unlocking and of self-creation that uses all systems as tools to re-write the script from the inside. The imagination is where the all-powerful potential of chaos spirals outward and creates a world. Each one of us as children generated a whole universe in our heads. The fact that the world is as apparently consistent as it is, is a testament to our occult powers, as the stochastic cosmos of probability becomes a world of predictability and even certainty. It is within the imagination that we are liberated or dammed. Everything you experience is modelled first in imaginative astral mind stuff and projected inward into our physiology, and then outward into the apparent universe. All the objects, experiences, events and behaviours we notice are organised and mapped primarily by the imagination. That is why, if we want a revolution, this process must begin inside our heads. For the imagination is the inner space in which all the greatest and most terrible possibilities are enfolded - the dream of Lascaux is here, and the horror of Year Zero, compassion and the gas chamber emerge from this same matrix. Our belief is that it is within the imagination that our fight against the hegemony of neo-liberal capitalist violence must begin, and magick shall be our weapon. Through understanding and beginning to operate consciously and beautifully within the imaginal space, we can liberate all our species. It is the imagination that provides us with empathy, the knowledge that I am like, yet different from you. It is the lack of this empathy, the poverty of the imagination that leads to exploitation and ennui. Our imagination is a limitless space, where we can create anything - through magick we can dare to create a utopia, a Garden of Earthly Delights right here, right now.

An account of my first journey with Santo Daime

(The following is a letter that I wrote to a friend after my first encounter with Daime.)

Well – what a fascinating weekend! I finally got a chance to try ayahuasca which, I'm certain you know, is one of the sacred South American shamanic drugs. It's a combination of two plants, one 'the vine of the soul' providing an MAO inhibitor and the other component of the potion is rich in vision-inducing DMT. DMT, which is found in lots of plants, is a very powerful psychedelic (with a quality reminiscent of magic mushrooms) but isn't orally active unless MAO inhibitors (themselves psychedelic at the correct dose) are taken simultaneously.

The setting for the experiment was a large warehouse in London where the Santo Daime church meet. I had the good fortune to be invited to the ceremony by my friend S. who I know through ceremonial magickal work. I met him and his partner at their house and drove over to the location of the ritual. The only indication that anything odd was being held inside was the large X-Files style grey blow-up space alien attached over the doorway of the warehouse.

Inside, I was met at the door, paid my dues for the ritual and bought a couple of hymn books which I knew would be important for the 'work' (as they call it).

Everyone was dressed in white (myself included) the Santo Daime colour (a few of the men also wore dark blue trousers and blue neckties which is also traditional garb). A few people sported sheriff style stars, which seemed to indicate some level of involvement or commitment to the group. The warehouse was a pretty welcoming environment with white wall hangings, gentle coloured lights, a small kitchen area at the back, toilets etc.

The girders holding up the roof were covered with silver foil. This, and some huge white sofas, gave the impression that I was entering a rather pleasant, relaxed space vehicle, which, in a sense, was true…

I got a brief chance to chat with a few people and acknowledge my nervous feelings (which was helpful), and by about 8pm everyone was assembled and it was time for the work to begin.

The lights were lowered and the two lead-musicians stood at the head of the altar (one with a guitar, the other a keyboard). Men sat in rows, on cushions, on one side of the low table (which was covered with a white cloth featuring a two barred cross, a candle and one or two other items of 'Catholic' paraphernalia), and women on the other.

A short prayer was said, then an 'Our Father...' and 'Hail Mary...' both in Portuguese and also in English. Then the 'Daime', the ayahuasca, was poured from a big plastic container into a jug and brought round for each participant by S. I was offered a shot glass full of the brownish, gravy looking mixture, took it and nodded thanks to S., made a little internal prayer myself to the spirit of ayahuasca and drank it down.

A few days before, I'd been talking to a friend from a magickal order in Brighton who had recently taken ayahuasca. He'd told me how, contrary to many reports, he'd really liked the taste and overall feel of the drink. I felt just the same, my fear about taking it had finally been overcome, I'd drunk the brew and, knowing psychedelics, knew there was no way out. I had to just relax and let it happen. Moreover the taste really wasn't that bad, bitter certainly (rather like wormwood tea) but not what I'd consider as particularly nasty. I was also lucky in that I didn't get any of the nausea that can be associated with ayahuasca (some people did vomit but there were buckets all round the room and vomiting is considered to be a purging of sin or dis-ease in the Santo Daime belief system).

We sat together in silence for about 20 minutes. I watched the musicians roll their heads, obviously feeling the onset of the drug. Then the lights were switched on giving us a fairly bright environment and one of the musicians said 'we'll start with hymn 10 in the blue book'. And so the singing began.

Each of the songs have been channelled from the Daime spirit and pretty much all the songs have the same one, two, three – four rhythm. They are sung in Portuguese (though the first hymn books we used also featured English translations).

One musician played an organ, the other a guitar (with other people drumming, and some keeping time with rattles). I used a rattle myself and this gave me a good focus for my attention as the first effects came on.

The songs kept going and I was finding it pretty easy to follow the hymns at first. Looking around I could see (across the altar) a few women yawning and some nervous shaking going on – two of the first signs of ayahuasca's effects. Then, as I looked at the page, I began to find the text swimming in a classic 'you're coming up on acid' kind of a way. I checked myself but couldn't feel any nausea, but was beginning to notice that something was definitely starting to happen.

This drug was different from others that I've tried. For as I felt myself entering a psychedelic state I didn't feel disconnected from my body or the environment. Whether it was the result of the ritual itself or the chemicals (or, as I suspect, both) I remained grounded and in my body for the duration of the trip.

Eventually the words on the page stabilised and I was left in a really odd state, a kind of double consciousness. I was simultaneously aware of the world around me, the faces of other worshippers, the building I was in, and yet I was also in a different place, a sort of dream land where DMT-like visuals (rather like mushroom visuals of green and purple geometric forms) rotated and danced. Eventually these forms became pictures and events, and yet I was still standing in the warehouse, holding my hymnbook and trying my best to sing in Portuguese.

The atmosphere was a strange and wonderful combination of a rave, a religious meeting and an occult ritual. Occasionally I'd glance around and see somebody sitting at the back of the room, chilling out and quietly meditating. One guy spent some time lying down in the row of people in front of me, moving around in the throws of what looked like a range of pleasurable psychedelic images/sensations. I certainly felt at home in my body (though my skin seemed to be subtly anaesthetised).

Experienced members of the church seemed to be taking it in turns to sit at the edge of the men and women's spaces where they could see everyone and help out if anyone was having a difficult time with the drug. As it was, only a couple of people were sick and they seemed to handle that fine themselves. Some others spent more or less time sitting or lying at the back or side of the main body of worshippers, entranced by their visions.

After a while (maybe an hour or so) we had another glass of Daime, and this one really topped up the experience for me. Still sitting on the floor and following the hymns, I found that I was simultaneously being 'investigated' by a female-insect-vegetative-computer-entity! This marvellous being descended from the ceiling, all grey and green and in a pleasant voice inquired who I was and what I was doing. This was, I realised, the spirit of the Daime, the 'Virgin of the Forest' (as the Daimeists call her) and she was taking a gentle interest in me.

I had the powerful feeling that the voice and form of the entity was created from the memories and raw neural wiring of my own mind, but that the spirit animating the mental creation was definitely something 'other', not part of me (except in a grand metaphysical sense) but an objective, external being.

There was then a brief break where we smoked some Santa Maria (neat cannabis joints) which had the effect of initially relaxing me and bringing on even deeper sensations. By now the drug seemed to have three powerful components, the first (the harmaline of the vine) a deep base note, a being-in-the-body and a solidity (this quality is called 'the force' by the Daimeists). Then there was the DMT-like visuals (known as 'the light') and between these two points (assisted by the relaxing effect of the Santa Maria) was a wonderful 'heart chakra' thing – a real MDMA sense of love, of beatitude, of calm joy.

Then back to more singing and later a further small dose of Daime. The musicians managed wonderfully to keep singing and playing, and with the occasional grin, giggle and whispered "so which number are we on?" I managed to keep up with the songs. The singing and the physical format of the ritual space (the rows of men and women facing each other, the central altar) helped stop my mind spinning off into neurotic psychedelic patterns (it's easy to get obsessed in those states with distractions: 'what's that funny noise?' 'My hands feel weird', 'something is wrong...' etc and get locked into an obsessive, even paranoid trip).

Another short break and more ganja then we cleared the floor and it was time to start dancing. The dance is done in lines/rows, with men facing the women across the altar. The basic step was the same one, two, three – four, rhythm moving from side to side. I really got into this, focusing on the hymnbook, moving step by step in a really weird psychedelic trance (especially after the final snifter of Daime). Unlike many trance experiences where all I can do is lie still, I was able to be in my body, in a room, filled with love and light and also aware of subtle visual changes and a kind of dreamscape, which was sometimes overlaid on the world. The effect was like my first experience of smoked DMT, where I could see the real world, but it was as though a dreamlike film was being projected over the objects in the room. I was awake and dreaming at the same time.

The night progressed and I found myself in the second row back from the altar, feeling happy and even proud that I had danced throughout the sessions. There was a final song, during which all the participants were encouraged to come together, and the ritual was closed.

With a final 'Our Father...' and 'Hail Mary...' in both Portuguese and English, the ritual was done.

I embraced the men around me and the group fell to talking. Some people went outside to smoke and I helped myself to some of the wonderful food that was available at the back of the warehouse. I got a chance to speak to some of the women I'd met before the ceremony and inevitably everyone was really friendly. I also found myself much more lucid and grounded much faster than with other powerful psychedelics. Sitting outside the back of the building, watching the sunrise I could talk and describe my impressions and feelings easily.

After maybe an hour I rejoined my friends and we drove back through the Sunday morning quiet streets of London to their flat where I slept for a few hours. I rested well and felt fine when I woke up.

Then it was time to head south to Brighton in order to do some filming for a magickal project concerning time sorcery, but that, as they say, is another story...

Sex, Drugs and Enlightenment

(A lecture I gave at Crowley Night, organised by the Silver Star Associates, in Brighton.)

Aleister Crowley, the Great Beast, Brother Perdurabo, Bafometh, the Wanderer of the Wastes - poet, writer, chess master, world-class mountaineer, linguist and, of course, magickian.

Over fifty years after the Great Beast was cremated in a ceremony that Brighton Council described as being 'unfortunately blasphemous', his legacy lives on. Crowley remains as relevant a countercultural icon today as ever.

In fact the popularity of the Beast is growing. As the demands of a generation of Willow-inspired teenage witches have caused the mind, body & spirit section of Waterstones to swell almost to bursting, last year saw the publication of two new biographies of Crowley. Right here in Brighton there are plans to launch a theatre production featuring the Beast (and this won't be the first time the character of the Beast has been a subject for a play) and in the new Alan Moore movie 'From Hell' the atmosphere is thickly laded with Crowleyian magick (Crowley gets a cameo in the graphic novel which I sincerely hope is left in by the filmmakers).

Now I suspect the majority of those people here are familiar with at least some of the reasons for Uncle Crowley's popularity. As a larger than life character, Crowley outraged, scandalised and generally poked fun at what he saw as the repressed and hypocritical values of Victorian Britain. If not exactly a thorn in the side of the establishment, he was at least part of the decadent flood that threatened to overwhelm the overt values of his time. As western culture has become more secular, more rational, so a shadow is cast, a shadow in which dwell characters like Crowley.

Outside of the field of magick, Crowley remains very much a 20th century icon, standing for rebellion against the constraints of social prudery. Crowley was into experimentation, sex, and drugs. Within occultism Crowley remains the most influential occultist of the 20th

the unknown and helped open the way, bringing back the shamanic use of drugs into our culture.

Today DMT, 2-CB, heroin, cocaine, mushrooms, ibogaine, LSD, ecstasy, Ayhuasaca, ketamine, cannabis - all these drugs have played a role in the exploration of the mystery of existence - an exploration where the aim is 'know thyself and unto thine own self be true' - what Crowley called 'The Great Work', discovering one's True Will.

In the 60's LSD helped rip apart the fabric of middle America. In the 90's psychonauts trafficked with entities found at the peak of the DMT trip, and every week millions of people on this planet use MDMA to have fun, relax and dance themselves into a trance of joy…

Crowley would have approved.

Crowley himself first started putting his lifelong interest in spirituality and drugs together when he was hanging out with a guy called Alan Bennett. Bennett was one of the first people to bring eastern Buddhist traditions to the west. Together they explored a variety of different magickal and yogic systems, using drugs as a perfectly legitimate way of enhancing and supporting their explorations.

Crowley also encountered the use of drugs in a spiritual context during his travels, particularly in India. Indeed hashish, which is used by many holy men and women in India, was to be one of the triggers that helped Crowley attain his first experience of Samadhi - a peak state of meditative consciousness.

Crowley was a great one for experiments and this is perhaps why, for magickians, he remains so fascinating, because he was always 'up for it', always ready to try a new sexual variation, a new belief system, a new pharmaceutical. Crowley was certainly well inside the realm of the shaman when he became one of the first Europeans to use mescaline. There is an apparently apocryphal story that it was Crowley who gave Aldous Huxley his first hit of mescaline. What is certainly the case is that in many rituals Crowley used a sacramental drink of mescaline - he attributed mescaline to the planet Mercury, an attribution that is concurred with by indigenous cultures in the Americas that use mescaline rich cacti in their rites. Mercury is of course, the healer, the guide, the trickster, and the shaman.

But of course one lesson of the trickster is that anyone can come a cropper (even the master), and Crowley certainly did in his relationship with some drugs, particularly heroin and cocaine. Indeed, Crowley spent a fair amount of time trying to break (with mixed results) his dependence on both drugs.

And it is in just this way that Crowley fits into the role of shaman.

Typically the shaman is the 'wounded healer', one who has gone down into the depths and often experienced a symbolic death. Both in his fight to break his drug addictions and deliberately in his own magickal work, Crowley sought to go down into these depths, into the 'long dark night of the soul'.

In Sicily in 1920, Crowley set up an esoteric commune 'the Abbey of Thelema' at Cefalu. Here he created 'The Chamber of Nightmares'. This room, which served as Crowley's bedroom, was covered with a range of disturbing murals, images of darkness, corruption and death. The names of these paintings included: *Morbid Hemaphrodite from Basutoland, Four degenerates between Christian and Jew, The Devil our Lord*. In this way Crowley was creating for himself an environment where he could generate just the kind of psychological and spiritual breakdown that is an essential process in the shamanic journey. The shaman descends to the depths, beyond revulsion, beyond the constraints of history and culture, into a symbolic death. Here in this world, within the womb of the dark, devouring mother, within the circle of the goddess Kali, the shaman is flayed alive, deconstructed. This death creates the possibility of a new birth so that the shaman can return from the darkness with magickal powers – with pleasure, freedom and power.

Crowley habitually inhabited the Chamber of Nightmares with his then 'Scarlet Woman', or Priestess, Leah Hirsig. Crowley's relationships with women were inevitably difficult. Here we have a man who, on one hand comes from a fundamentalist, upper class background (with all the inherent snobbery, sexism and racism that that implies), and yet he knows, as a shaman, that in order to find his power he must die into the feminine, into the darkness, into the great Black Goddess. The strain of

29

these paradoxical roles can certainly be seen in Crowley's writing – one moment he is being quite radical in his understanding of women and the sacred feminine as a whole, the next he is babbling sexist drivel of the worst order.

Crowley was certainly aware of the importance of Woman (but perhaps not women) within the occult tradition. His channelled 'Book of the Law' makes the character of the Scarlet Women, and the sacred female (represented by the Goddesses Nuit and Babalon) central to his Thelemic mythology. In this reconsecration of the power of the feminine Crowley is certainly acting as a shaman – going beyond the boundaries of his culture to re-establish the sacred female.

Shamanism also often involves the use of power animals or totem animals, beings with whom the shaman makes a bargain to gain power, or to be guided through a territory of the spirit world. For Crowley these animal guides took the form of the physical women that were his magickal and sexual partners - perhaps the universe having a joke at the expense of some of Crowley's more sexist views! A glance at his diaries shows that for many of his more important initiations and explorations, women that Crowley gave magickal animal names to - 'The Camel', 'The Ape' , 'The Dog' 'The Cat and 'The Snake'- played key roles.

Crowley also has to wrestle with his own sexual orientation. Like many shamans he was bisexual (as a person 'between the worlds') but again the cultural conditions of late 19th and early 20th century society didn't make this situation easy. Like many shamans Crowley explored the possibility of examining his homosexual desires by creating a female alter ego 'Alys'. In some cultures the shaman is said to be of a third sex. For instance, in some Native American nations sacred transvestites exist within the culture who have a especially strong medicine because they are again creatures of the borders, between the realms of male and female.

Also essential to the form of Crowley's magick, just as in shamanism, was a tree. The Qabalah, the Hebrew Tree of Life, was a key element of 19th century occultism, the systems of which Crowley had absorbed through his studies within the Golden Dawn.

The tree forms the framework, the map, within which much of Crowley's magick takes place. As a glyph of the whole universe the Qabalah asserts that, however occult the connections, all things in the universe are connected. This series of connections gives rise to the idea of correspondence – the poetic process whereby every phenomenon is related to every other.

For Crowley the shaman, drugs, as one of the principle tools of exploration in the innerworlds, could be attributed to various areas and stages on the Tree. Each sphere or branch of the tree of life could be linked to a planetary force. So along with his attribution of Mescaline to Mercury, Crowley describes opium as being related to the sphere of Jupiter, Tobacco to Mars, Alcohol to the Sun. In this way a poetic psychotopography is created, describing the relationship of drug states to the occult forces of the universe.

Like the World Ash Tree of Norse mythology, for Crowley the Qabalah remained the *axis mundi*, the central glyph around which the rest of his magickal tradition developed. Indeed Crowley saw his magickal career directly in terms of the Qabalah, as a series of initiations, moving from branch to branch of this sacred tree.

Crowley is also a shaman in that he is a trickster, as anybody familiar with his writing will acknowledge. There are jokes and glib remarks nestled side-by-side with jewels of wisdom and erudite esoteric observations. Like the shaman, Crowley is half holy guru and half insane madman. As a writer, his CV contains great works of esoteric genius as well as pornographic limericks. As an experimenter with sex, he came from a hugely repressive background and tried to free himself from sin by sinning all he could. As an explorer of drugs, he showed how drugs could be used in a magickal context and also provides an object lesson in the pain of drug addiction.

Now, years after his death, Crowley continues to play the shamanic role. The shaman in a tribal culture helps to link together the world of culture and the world of nature, of humans and the gods. In just this way Crowley stands as a link between the occult tradition that survived two millennia of Christian rule and the emerging threads of magick in the modern period. Between the Masonic style of formalised Golden Dawn ceremony and the modern rituals of Witches, Chaos Magickians, freestyle Pagans, shamans and Thelemites is the figure of Uncle Crowley. Crowley was one of the central characters who helped the re-membering of the occult tradition. Along with people such as Dion Fortune, Spare and McGregor Mathers, Crowley helped gather up the isolated fragments of our occult heritage and mould these into a coherent, growing, modern body of knowledge.

Crowley's emphasis is always on experiment, on practice over theory and on trying magick for yourself. Crowley's system of Thelema declares that it uses 'The method of science', with 'the aim of religion', and so Crowley seeks to bridge, with magick, the great gap between these two apparently irreconcilable aspects of the modern human experience.

A shaman is somebody who stands in this liminal space, the space between the worlds. This is the space that magick has always occupied. It is the space that drugs occupy, a shadowy world between the legal and illegal, the sacred and profane. Drugs and magick can raise the individual to the greatest peaks of ecstasy and enlightenment and plunge the user into the most unholy of hells.

When I wrote *Pharmakon* I have to say that Aleister was never very far from my thoughts. When you explore the use of drugs in an esoteric context you just can't help acknowledging Crowley. It was Crowley who formed the foundation upon which the explorations of Leary, McKenna, Lilly and many, many more have been founded. Crowley showed that sex and drugs are a vital part of the magickal project, that if you're going to explore yourself and the mystery of existence, then these tools are as legitimate as solitary mediation and fasting.

So Crowley is, in one of his forms, the shaman – the trickster, the wounded healer, the magickian who descends into the depths and brings back a new revitalised magick to his tribe, the man who is guided through the labyrinth of the dark goddess by his female, animal companions, a link between the magick of the past and of the future.

Crowley the shaman stands in the liminal space, in the twilight place between the worlds, urging us to experiment, to explore, to discover, to engage with passion the mystery of existence – to dare to live!

Daring to live just like you – you excellent people! Thank you.

Ra-Hoor-Khuit Ritual

(This ritual was performed in a nursery school attached to a liberal Christian church in Sussex.)

Personnel preparation:

Participants are asked to do the following:

To fast for 12 hours prior to the ritual

To abstain from orgasm for 12 hours before the ritual

To spend at least 30 minutes in meditation for five nights prior to the ritual, focused on the following concepts:

In Aikido when an attacker approaches one should step forward. To step closer to an attacker means that there will be less energy behind any strike.

When fighting it is important to be able to blend with one's adversary, indeed to see that adversary as a partner, another dancer in the duet of conflict. The aim is to hold the centre of the dance, to move with the ease of a fluid fire – then to act, to make a small change, a Willed alteration in the form of the dance, to win.

When we strike we should strike hard and fast.

In this age of the child we fear pain – what good, we ask, is suffering? But cannot suffering, not as martyrdom, but as simple difficulty and work, be good? Is the pain of deep massage, of labour, of piercing without value? Is suffering not a mark of being alive?

We have undertaken, as a group, a number of rituals of the 'red path' – The River out of Eden, devotions to Kali in the muladhara, the exploration of fear through Sufi spinning, the slaying of the Bull. By this rite we can seek to integrate all these things, to allow the red power to ignite within all who participate in this ritual.

We seek:

Integrity, Definition of our Wills, Success in New Projects, Success in Battles, the Burning up of that which is Not Needed, Courage, Determination, Strength, Health, Vigour, Rich Sexuality, Removal of all Obstacles, Skill in the Charging of Talismans, Overcoming the Illusion of Omnipotence, The Power of Commanding Demons, Protection from Accidents, Skill in working with technology, Protection in Travel, Reward and joy in our Work, Knowledge of our limits, Understanding of the Laws of the Universe, Stamina in Our Labour.

What are you prepared to fight for?

* * *

If you are attending the ritual please wear red and/or black if possible. Any suitable Martian offering for the altar space would be appreciated. Please do not turn up before 8pm on the night as Sister QOFE and I will still be setting up.

Things for the ritual

Aeon/6 wands/empress.

Red flowers

RHK sculpture

Incense and burner

Horseshoe

Scourge

Chain

Red altar cloth

String to make pentagram and protractor

Wine

Vessel for wine

Bell and knife

Sword

Lots of candles/red lamps/salt for pentagram

Music system and pre-recorded ritual music (15 mins drumming building slightly, then 5 key sounds – on the fifth the energy is released)..

Praxis

The temple is prepared according to the plan devised by Julian.

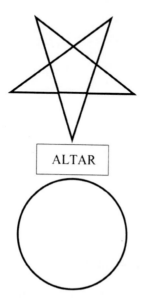

Participants begin in the circle and, when they have past the Ordeal move beyond the altar to stand around the pentagram.

Begin by shaking out energy and stretching, using the sun salute.

Then focus on the person opposite you, and imagine a sun, a star burning in their heart, enveloping and surrounding them with power.

Bring your hands up, palms facing outward until you can sense the energy of the people either side of you.

Now make your awareness wider to include the circle of stars of which you are one. As it expands outward it banishes all hindrance to our work, it flexes our character armour, it drives out any stray thoughts. AUM

We are the centre of the World!

(Explain format)

All stand before the altar of Geburah.

A bell is struck 6, 5.

A chant begins.

A ka dua

Tuf ur biu

B a'a chefu

Dudu ner af an nuteru

Each person comes forward to the altar and will be asked a question by The Priestess of Ma'at.

What is your name?

What are your prepared to fight for?

Are you willing to suffer to learn?

Those who pass the test will be scourged five times and will make an offering of incense to Ra-Hoor-Khuit.

When all participants are within the inner sanctum the chant will cease. Julian will give an invocation to Ra-Hoor-Khuit, with cries of Ra-Hoor-Khuit at the end of each line.

Ra-Hoor Khuit!

We call to you! (chorus: Ra Hoor Khuit!)

By your many names: (chorus: Ra Hoor Khuit!)

Horus, Tir, Ogun, Ares, Siva, Mars, Gawain (chorus: Ra Hoor Khuit!)

By your many forms! (chorus: Ra Hoor Khuit!)

Nike, Kali, Babalon, Sekhmet, Pomba Gira, Kundalini (chorus: Ra Hoor Khuit!)

Brilliant star, rising serpent! (chorus: Ra Hoor Khuit!)

We call on you! (chorus: Ra Hoor Khuit!)

Hawk headed god of this Age! (chorus: Ra Hoor Khuit!)

Bringer of Justice and swift retribution! (chorus: Ra Hoor Khuit!)

Fill us with your radiance! (chorus: Ra Hoor Khuit!)

God of agriculture, of the blood of the land! (chorus: Ra Hoor Khuit!)

Bringer of the Vision of Power! (chorus: Ra Hoor Khuit!)

Hawk headed redeemer! (chorus: Ra Hoor Khuit!)

Make us conscious of our own power! (chorus: Ra Hoor Khuit!)

Awaken us, awaken within us! Wake! (chorus: Ra Hoor Khuit!)

Inspire us to fight the fever of tyranny! (chorus: Ra Hoor Khuit!)

To oppose oppression, to burn up iniquity! (chorus: Ra Hoor Khuit!)

Maker of the Road of iron Will, (chorus: Ra Hoor Khuit!)

Blacksmith of the Logos, (chorus: Ra Hoor Khuit!)

Hawk eyed God who sees through all deception! (chorus: Ra Hoor Khuit!)

Burn up all that stands between us and the Great Work! (chorus: Ra Hoor Khuit!)

To Me! To Me! (chorus: Ra Hoor Khuit!)

Be with us this night. (chorus: Ra Hoor Khuit!)

Your breath fills our nostrils, (chorus: Ra Hoor Khuit!)

Your blood pumps in our muscles, (chrous: Ra Hoor Khuit!)

Your wisdom ignites in our minds, (chorus: Ra Hoor Khuit!)

Ra-Hoor-Khuit you are with us! (chorus: Ra Hoor Khuit!)

Be Here NOW! (chorus: Ra Hoor Khuit!)

All participants will then use the 'hawk breath' technique, this involves an open tai chi stance, breathing up energy and opening your arms like the wings of a hawk. Keep tension in the limbs. Breath out as the hands are lowered to the centre. This has the effect of flooding the body with oxygen and stimulating the spinal system. You may feel your spine getting hotter. During this, visualise the red energy building within your aura.

Once the energy has reached an appropriate pitch, it will be directed into a sacrament by flinging your arms out and with a cry, the energy will be discharged and ritually consumed. The peak will be indicated as the fifth sounding of a bell on the pre-recorded tape.

(Just before the peak, the priestess raises her sword and as the peak comes plunges it into the wine with a shriek.)

Toasts, banishing with laughter.

De-briefing.

Raising the River

Purpose - to re-energise the feminine energy in Brighton by symbolically raising the river, the Wellsbourne, that used to flow over ground from Patcham to the sea at Pool Valley (coach station).

This ritual includes an invocation of Brigid, the Anglo Saxon goddess of smithcraft, fire, creativity and inspiration. Brigid is the goddess after whom Brighton is named. Legend has it that the stones at the base of the fountain on the Steine are the remains of megaliths sacred to Brigid.

The image - as the river rises it unblocks the knots of masculine energy within the town and allows them to flow. The rising river is a re-emergence of the feminine, both as the caring sacred mother, and also as the goddess 'armed and militant', she seeks (like the flood waters) to purify and re-member. She is like the flooding Nile, destructive in some senses but giving rise to fertile new soil (part of the war memorial on the Steine is for those who died in Egypt).

The ritual - kindle a single flame in your home hearth, then walk down to the fountain on the Steine. Take a flame with you in the form of a lamp or lantern. The fountain you are journeying to is the Three of Cups - Abundance - the feminine as Binah (Brigid is the classic Triple Goddess, much like the classical Hekate). As you walk, imagine the power of the river raising up, the feminine force of the water in the landscape flooding down the hills of Brighthelmstone, washing away all restrictions. As you walk, chant, sing, give voice to your own stream of consciousness. If you feel self-conscious about this, try holding a mobile phone which allows you to create a Temporary Autonomous Personal Zone. Let your words come, be inspired. As you walk recognise that each feature within the landscape holds the possibility within it of a utopian Brighton, a free space where masculine and feminine powers can flow harmoniously together.

When we meet at the fountain we will then begin to circle the structure, invoking Brigid to raise the river. We will then all put our lamps down beside the fountain and leave them as offerings to the spirit of the river. Before we leave we will ceremonially share water.

There is, of course, nothing to stop people walking together or alone to the fountain. Participants may also choose to use other techniques to alter consciousness prior to making their walk.

The route that you choose could be something like a situationist dérive or drift, but this is not a movement through a meaningless landscape but instead a pilgrimage of intense meaningfulness. Go with the flow, allow your feet and thoughts to wander, and each time you see something that pisses you off, let the magick water of the raising river flow through it. In initial experiments I've found it helpful to use the keyword 'flow', so each time I wander past the Masonic hall on Queens road, I repeat the keyword and the visualisation of the rising river, rising female power in the town, washing away this phallocentric crap.

Psychogeography in action

We'd just returned from our presentation, pleased that our words and images had been so well received. Soror mill mill was in the audience.

We'd talked about Kali, shown the splendid interior of the Viaduct road temple and mother Helen had spoken of her labour. She told of how the Great Bear and Mamma Yemanja had embedded the birth of her baby in the web of symbolic meaning, enriching us with a dark fertility.

We'd spoken about psychogeography, showed a picture of the West Pier and talked about Iain Sinclair. Said that memory was the key.

On our return to the house all was still. Osric sleeping like an improbably beautiful doll in his cradle. We talked and sat on the kitchen step, smoking and laughing.

Finally it was time for Rose to go. Pulling on her woolly hat, we kissed and said our goodbyes.

Helen and I prepared for bed, Osric whimpering in his dreams. As I went to turn the living room light off I notice a glint of silver under a black cat. Rose's keys!

I picked them up and explained to Helen what I'd found, and asked her which way she would have gone. "Down Trafalgar Street", so I set off, running and watching.

As I ran down the hill I remember thinking that we should have called her. Typical. Here I was, running, using all this energy, if only I'd tried to think things through, to be a bit intelligent rather than just acting on impulse, we could have sorted the problem so easily!

Still, I ran down the hill, conscious I was moving fast, aware that Rose would probably be walking purposefully but not that quickly, a thin roll-up smouldering between her fingers. There was no sign of her.

I got down to the bottom of the valley, the end of London Road near the Hobgoblin. Frater rhino had seen a fight kick off there, Helen said that she thought it was a power spot, a kind of nasty, gnarly power, oppressed and waiting to burst out as violence.

41

No sign of Rose. I fingered the keys, uncertain. Should I go to Rose's house and wait? Head back? I'd no money in my pocket for a 'phone call. Arse.

I began to head back, mentally asking the Esu spirits (who seem to rule all things key related in my life) to help. As I re-crossed London Road I imagined a huge blue laguz rune and vibrated it's name. There it was at the end of the road, pouring blue watery healing energy into the place. Helen and I had raised another one two days before in St Anne's Wells Park near, where the healing well of Freya has dried up.

Looking left I saw a figure crossing the road, it was Rose. I ran after her and said something like "you may need these" offering her the keys. "Oh darling, bless you", she said "thanks". We parted, her the woman who has re-made herself through the power of this town. Rose, the youthful Hekate had been given her keys back as she stood on the underground river.

I ran back, cheerful. Back up the hill. On Trafalgar Street a young woman was walking down the road swinging fluorescent ribbons. Kids were skating what I suddenly realised would be a great road to ride down. The pub where our first Brighton IOT meeting was held was chucking out, and a few souls lingered in the doorway.

I could feel the city around me, feel that I have been and am living in this place. Feel the network of history, personal and collective, around me. I was aware of all those amazing, magickal, creative, excellent people whom I have come to know in this place.

And even though I was leaving (we are all leaving in our own individual ways) I felt the city as a source of strength, a nurturing mother who had supported me in so many ways.

Rose had her 'phone switched off anyway, Helen had tried to call her.

That night I dreamed of Hekate's Fountain

Oh self, where art thou?

No man is an island, entire of itself;
every man is a piece of the continent,
a part of the main.
If a clod be washed away by the sea,
Europe is the less,
as well as if a promontory were,
as well as if a manor of thy friend's or of thine own were.

Any man's death diminishes me
because I am involved in mankind;
and therefore never send to know for whom the bell tolls;
it tolls for thee. . . .

from Meditation 17 by John Donne, 1624

We, in the (post) industrialised West, live in the era of individualism. The stultifying duty and traditions that bound the generations before us have been hugely eroded. No longer will we unquestioning lay down our lives because the monarch decrees it. No more will we beat ourselves up with guilt if we disappoint our parents. We are individuals, self-determined, and we are free!

The picture of the self is of the economically independent, conscious 'I' that has free will and is, ultimately, responsible to no one but itself. We are the monad, the indivisible atom. Much of our society, our notions of identity, much of our concept of volition and most of our day-to-day being-in-the-world is based around the idea that the 'I' is the sovereign sanctuary. Our notions of rights and responsibilities (especially as they apply in matters of law) are predicated on the unitary self. Although I would not deny the virtue, especially in historical terms, of this emerging concept of the self, it is far from the whole picture. Indeed, so successful (for the last 200 years in the English speaking world) has this conception of the self become that it has created a psychic deformity in our culture.

Where, in the past, obligation and tradition were the bonds that forced people into servitude, today rank individualism is killing off empathy

From the Tiphereth stage onward, in Crowley's conception of the Qabalah, the grades of attainment become increasingly about a much broader sense of self. Following Tiphereth into Geburah, the Adeptus Major; "…establishes a new incarnation of deity; as in the legends of Leda, Semele, Miriam, Pasiphae, and others." That is create a new vehicle for the divine revelation or the unfolding of magickal power in the world. This might be a new Order or school of thought (or a child)."

Later at the Chesed grade of Adeptus Exemptus begins what within Thelema (if the Taoist elements of the system are to be appreciated fully) is the supreme attainment:

> "He {sic} must then decide upon the critical adventure of our Order; the absolute abandonment of himself and his attainments. He cannot remain indefinitely an Exempt Adept; he is pushed onward by the irresistible momentum that he has generated. Should he fail, by will or weakness, to make his self-annihilation absolute, he is none the less thrust forth into the Abyss; but instead of being received and reconstructed in the Third Order, as a Babe in the womb of our Lady BABALON, under the Night of Pan, to grow up to be Himself wholly and truly as He was not previously, he remains in the Abyss, secreting his elements round his Ego as if isolated from the Universe, and becomes what is called a "Black Brother." Such a being is gradually disintegrated from lack of nourishment and the slow but certain action of the attraction of the rest of the Universe, despite his now desperate efforts to insulate and protect himself, and to aggrandise himself by predatory practices. He may indeed prosper for a while, but in the end he must perish, especially when with a new Æon a new word is proclaimed which he cannot and will not hear, so that he is handicapped by trying to use an obsolete method of Magick, like a man with a boomerang in a battle where everyone else has a rifle."
>
> Crowley - *One Star In Sight*

Modern Thelemites, such as Rodney Orpheus, writing in *Abrahadabra*, echo this. Here is Orpheus musing on the meaning of the core Thelemic dictum "Do what thou wilt shall be the whole of the Law",

"...All things must change and grow, and a fixed moral code cannot grow with you. Only you can judge what action is right for you at any one time. To stop growing, to become rigid and unbending, is to start dying. As the ancient Chinese classic, the Dao De Jing puts it: "Rigidity and hardness are the stigmata of death; elasticity and adaptability, of life." And as Thelemites we embrace Life in our arms, we live to the fullest manner we are capable, and we extend our capabilities as much as possible, in order to be able to experience even more in the future. "Wisdom says: be strong! Then thou canst bear more rapture." - *Liber AL*."

But the dwellers in the Abyss that wish to 'stop growing, to become rigid and unbending' do exist. Such self-professed 'Black Brothers' include the 'Xeper' Setians. The term Xeper ('I have come into Being') is taken to suggest the full development of an unassailable self. Thus these Satanists are busy building up their egos and astral bodies in the hope that they can persist indefinitely. An Australian Setian temple declares on their website:

"One of the main focuses of the Temple is the Word of the Aeon of Set - "Xeper", an Ancient Egyptian word meaning "to become" or "I have come into Being". This is both watchword and an Initiatory focus - to become the best individual one is able to be, to become like the Prince of Darkness - an eternal independent entity, rather than the immersion of consciousness as proposed by White Magic and associated religious and philosophical schools."

Thus the dwellers in the Abyss hope to buy off that Might Demon Choronzon with whatever meagre offerings they can scrape together. They fear Babalon (the Goddess of Dissolution in Love) and her consort Baphomet (the Shiva Pan-Beast of the Will to Live). These Abyss Dwellers are the true vampires in our society, draining the unwary victim of power and creativity and love. This blood is captured in the unholy vessels of corporate capitalism, personality cults and post-industrial 'progress'. It is harvested as tribute to Choronzon so that the Black Brothers can persist against the flow of time and evolution. They spill the blood of others rather than their own, but this stratagem can hardly work forever.

"And this is the meaning of the Supper of the Passover, the spilling of the blood of the Lamb being a ritual of the Dark Brothers, for they have sealed up the Pylon with blood, lest the Angel of Death should enter therein. Thus do they shut themselves off from the company of the saints. Thus do they keep themselves from compassion and from understanding. Accurs'd are they, for they shut up their blood in their heart.

They keep themselves from the kisses of my Mother Babylon, and in their lonely fortresses they pray to the false moon. And they bind themselves together with an oath, and with a great curse. And of their malice they conspire together, and they have power, and mastery, and in their cauldrons do they brew the harsh wine of delusion, mingled with the poison of their selfishness.

Thus they make war upon the Holy One, sending forth their delusion upon men, and upon everything that liveth. So that their false compassion is called compassion, and their false understanding is called understanding, for this is their most potent spell. Yet of their own poison do they perish, and in their lonely fortresses shall they be eaten up by Time that hath cheated them to serve him, and by the mighty devil Choronzon, their master, whose name is the Second Death 11, for the blood that they have sprinkled on their Pylon, that is a bar against the Angel Death, is the key by which he entereth in."

Crowley – The Vision and The Voice.

This drive to buttress the monad of self against the flow of change in the universe leads to some curious outcomes. Many 'Xepherites' don't smoke dope because drugs destabilise the boundaries of the ego. Ironically the most 'satanic' of modern occultists may also be some of the most sober! Our fearsome 'black magickians' are whiter-than-white! (Rather than use the term 'Black Brother' perhaps 'Bloodless Adept' would be better, for blackness suggests Alchemical richness, fertility and therefore putrefaction and change.)

This kind of 'bloodless' self-protectionism is also seen in groups like the Extropians, where behind the 'onwards and upwards' rhetoric of the 5 Extropian principles (Boundless Expansion, Self-Transformation,

Dynamic Optimism, Intelligent Technology & Spontaneous Order) there lurks terror of entropy, of limitation, of dissolution, of death. Thus the Extopians seek to download themselves out of the tiresome (and tire-able) 'wet-ware' of the body and into the eternal, infinitely malleable world of virtual reality.

In the chaos current also we can see traces of this desire to create an eternal, unbreakable self. In 'Liber Null' Carroll provides a series of rituals (the Red, White and Black Rites) which are intended to allow the adept to transfer their consciousness intact from body to body. This is variously achieved by the reincarnatory highjacking of a new body, or through a direct transplanting of consciousness from one bodily vehicle to another (through murder and mutilation). Leaving aside the questionable effectiveness of these rituals, they can certainly be seen as fulfilling the mission of the 'Bloodless Adepts'.

Carroll's work as well as the musings of the Extropian movement clearly suggest that the self is not presumed to be identical with the body in any way and that an ego can meaningfully be downloaded or transferred from the fleshy casing (either to silicone chips or a new body) without making much difference.

There are a number of obvious problems with this belief, not least of which is that philosophical schools such as Phenomenology clearly articulate that much of our sense of self is predicated on our actual bodies. Some AI researchers who believe that the reason we have human-shaped consciousness is that we have human-shaped bodies hold a similar view. Much of our conception of the world arises from the fact that most of us have two hands, eyes at the top of our bodies, the need to sleep etc. A mind, and certainly a human self, downloaded into a machine would very quickly change from the self that occupies the 'wet-ware' into something quite different. Quite what would happen to a conscious, adult self trapped in the body of a new born baby is impossible to say but madness and then protective amnesia (of one's former existence as an adult consciousness) might be expected. These kinds of changes to the self are not what the Bloodless Adept is aiming for. The process of change, however we cut it, is inevitable, as Crowley says, "Such a being is gradually disintegrated from lack of nourishment and the slow but certain action of the attraction of the rest of the Universe."

Indeed simple cellular biology shows the lie of the monad self. We experience our bodies as 'ours', yet more than 50% of the cells that make up our bodies themselves are 'not self', they are the flora and fauna of our guts, the tiny mushroom-like structures that sprout from our eye lashes, the virtually independent mitochondrial bodies that lurk within cells. Away from the physical stuff of the body and into the realm of the mind; children interviewed at the age of 7 were asked a series of questions; Who were their heroes? What did they want to be when they grew up? Where would they like to travel? The same individuals interviewed in their early 30s had only a slightly higher than chance ability to guess (or recall) what their answers were twenty-odd years earlier. So our self is the apparent continuity of conscious content rather than the literal bits of information that are stored (mostly irretrievably) in our memories. However, as I said above, we cannot simply dismiss the self (like a 1950s behaviourist dismissing the existence of consciousness because it cannot be located and measured). Instead, we must propose a model of the self that acknowledges our embodied nature and allows for us to reach beyond our individual 'machines'.

Such a way of thinking about the self, that draws on a number of esoteric and quantum physics ideas, is that of the self as field, a network that partly 'lives' inside our bodyminds and is partly contained in the contextual interactions between us and Others. A very accessible description of such a model can be found in *The Quantum Self* by Danah Zohar. A reviewer of Zohar's work explains, "…the book's main thrust is to knock down our notions of the separate Self. Quantum mechanics overthrows the cosmos of sovereign objects separated in space - the Aspect experiment confirmed that outlandish quantum prediction that 'everything is connected' in a real and measurable sense. So if we are quantum entities, what of our separateness? Zohar makes the case for an overlapping, connected, mutually engaged world of I-and-we rather than seeing individuals as isolated islands of being. Surely a positive counter to a world where we are only united in our roles as producers & consumers."

For magickians, this notion of a self that is non-local in space but never the less rooted in the peculiar quantum properties of neural tissue is a very appealing one. It supports the 'all things are interconnected' dictum of magick and gives value to the body as the receiver (or transceiver) of consciousness (and modifier of its contents). The idea that empathy and sensitivity to others is not a weakness of the monad self but an appreciation that 'I' am something greater than my own desires has many magickal implications. One of the most obvious is that it provides an esoteric ethic, one that does not conflict with Crowley's Thelema directly but places the emphasis on a more Maatian style relationship of the individual Star to the rest of the cosmos.

Moreover, such a model of the self is supportive in a broader sense of the project of being a magickian. Magick is the technology of the imagination, and the everyday human effect of a developed imagination is empathy (see my work on autism and schizophrenia in *Pharmakon* for a detailed discussion of this process). Without empathy we become automata, unable to make the leap across the 'imaginative discontinuity', to recognise that my internal world is similar and yet different from yours. We become increasingly impotent in the imaginative realm if we see the self as a fixed atomic point existing independently of our relations with others. Ethically, rather than standing up for our brothers and sisters we keep our heads down, on the pretext that what is going on is 'nothing to do with me' and close ourselves up in Black Brotherhood. Without our empathic imaginations we make a false crown of Daath and reject love as soppy and weak. Rather than realising our fullest potential we have lost our basic humanity.

The quantum self model leads to a natural Greater Vehicle position and a compassion for other beings. Rather than isolating our magickal being from others and characterising them (or indeed aspects of ourselves) as 'monkeys' or 'robots' (terms often used within R.A.Wilson-eque literature), we can imagine all of our individual consciousnesses as elements within a great continuum. Certainly, in terms of processes such as initiatory events, there may be radical discontinuities between aspects of one's self, between periods in one's history or between oneself and others, yet the underlying shared non-local nature of consciousness *per se* remains. Such a position is more likely to encourage the illuminated adept to become a teacher and guide, rather than a sad misanthrope.

A magickal worldview founded on a quantum view of the self is more likely to be life affirming, less willing to bow to Choronzon. Such a worldview is also able to create a positive theme or purpose for one's incarnation. Such a sense of purpose may be multi-vocal, highly flexible or general, such as Crowley's "existence is pure joy", or his notion that the aim of life is to pursue one's 'True Will'. Such a coherent worldview staves off the viral-meme servitor of post-modern ennui and provides:

> "— a theme which integrates the sense of self, the sense of self and others, and the sense of how these relate to the wider world – to Nature and other creatures, to the environment as a whole, to the planet, the universe, and ultimately to God – to some overall purpose and direction... A successful worldview must, in the end, draw all these levels – the person, the social, and the spiritual – into one coherent whole. If it does so, the individual has access to some sense of who he is, why he is here, how he relates to others, and how it is valuable to behave."
>
> Danah Zohar - *The Quantum Self*

In terms of a magickal notion of evolution or development (the downward motion toward the root of Kether proposed in the Western magickal tradition) the quantum sense of self enlarges us as we live. Rather than seeing death as something to fear and to fend off with anything from life extension technologies to abominable rites, we can see death as the moment at which our self ceases to operate within the context of the bodymind and becomes part of the non-local nature of quantum consciousness. In other words, when we die we live on in the field of consciousness (memory) of others. Thus in the 'final' Ipsissimus initiation, where the microcosm and macrocosm are unified, the 'I' becomes 'We', one changes from 'being' (Xepher) to 'doing' (Ankh 'to go or move'). Pete Carroll explores this process of the collapse of the subject/object divide in *Liber Kaos* with the notion of V-Prime (text in which all instance of the verb 'to be' are removed'), or as the Rasta says, "as Brethren we is 'I and I'".

> "The Ipsissimus has no relation as such with any Being: He has no will in any direction, and no Consciousness of any kind involving

duality, for in Him all is accomplished; as it is written "beyond the Word and the Fool, yea, beyond the Word and the Fool."

Crowley - One Star In Sight

This lack of duality, or rather the resolution of duality through the ecstatic process of unity, is the peak experience of magick. Obviously we might consider this as the one-off moment of one's own death, or we might imagine it as a series of ecstatic moments, a necklace of pearls of unity and division. As Crowley expresses it writing as Nuit in *Liber AL*, "For I am divided for love's sake, for the chance of union". In either case the self/other divide is collapsed in order to produce this ecstatic event (the word ecstasy itself meaning literally to stand outside of one's self).

So what are we left with? With a self that comes into being through interaction, that is rooted in the body but also exists as the context of interactions in a non-local field of consciousness. Indeed this consciousness need no longer be a solely human preserve, and so we are back to the occult *anima vitae* where all things in the universe are conscious. The self is an apparent property of this non-local consciousness when it is 'contained' within a specific identifiable body. It has an individual history but is predicated on its relationship with others. No Other = No Self.

Ethically the quantum self paradigm demonstrates that we are fundamentally interdependent on others: for food, love, language, care and indeed the very existence of our apparently separate consciousnesses. This echoes the simple fact that none of us would have made it past childhood were it not for the care of others (however good, bad or indifferent). Whilst we may harp on about our own True Wills, if we do so in such a way that we are really buoying up our own egos we really have missed the point. If we choose to believe in the Aeon of Horus we should remember that any child, no matter how Crowned and Conquering, needs carers to help it grow to its fullest potential. Every sovereign Star is only one in the multitude of the body of Nuit.

And as for those Bloodless Adepts, those Black Brothers sitting growing dusty in the abyss, withholding their life force against the mighty wheel of change, I bless them. May Babalon have compassion for them when their turn to sup at her cup finally comes.

53

Web resources.

www.io.com/~khabir/onestar2.html

www.xeper.org

www.extropy.org

www.rodneyorpheus.de/abrahadabra/index.html

www.meta-religion.com/Physics/Quantum_physics/
quantum_self.htm

www.beyondthenet.net/misc/science4.htm

On becoming a father

It's curious, like the effect of a datura trip, how the memory of labour and birth disappears. More for my partner than for me, it is as if some system in the mind closes over, locks away the memory of that powerful experience. So part of my reason for writing this essay is to reconnect, to provide on paper, at least, a pathway to the events of 29-30th June 2002, the day that my son was born. The second reason is to contextualise the event of becoming a father in a magickal sense. I believe that one of the key reasons for magickal practice is to help us re-enchant our lives, to link our individual realities into something greater - The Pattern, the Great Work, the Tao. Within the Western Magickal Tradition it is easy to mistake the map for the territory, to assume that one is only doing magick when in a circle surrounded by all the bells and smells of ceremonial work. But as Austin Spare says, one of the reasons for doing magick is 'to intensify the normal', to make us richer in breadth and depth of experience.

I recall that, in early 2001, Brother Kondawani and I were talking about his work with the Ori, a principle from the African tradition that incorporates ideas that are similar to the notion of the True Will or Holy Guardian Angel in Occidental symbolism. Brother K had set up an altar to help him focus on his work with the Ori, which incorporated photographs of his ancestors. I remember him saying that, within the African traditions, the ancestors are seen as very significant in terms of one's own spiritual development. 'We tend to think, hey my grandparents never did any magick, so what about them? They don't really matter, they're not cool', he explained.

Making connections with one's literal ancestors, rather than a mythological notion of 'the ancestors' helps to bring the process of self-exploration right home, to make it concrete. Later that year, in my own work with the Ori I dreamt about my grandmother (who I had watched die earlier in the year) and added a photo of her to the altar I was working with. My grandmother was not a magickian, in fact towards the last few years of her life we had little contact and I must confess that there were lots of things (including her working class racism) that I did not like about her. Still, she was my grandmother and as such is part of my story. Coming to see the worth of her as a person, the wisdom that she did have, the

letting the sensations, which were like period pains move through her. I phoned the delivery suite at about midnight and explained that we were booked in for a home birth and that my partner was in labour. They told me to 'phone again once she was having contractions at the rate of one every 3 minutes and this rate had been sustained for at least and hour.

I think I was fairly calm at this point. Indeed, in some ways I was looking forward to Helen's labour in as much as I'm pretty good in most crisis situations and actively enjoy being able to gently manage difficult processes. The few times I've needed to talk people down who have panicked when on drugs, I have really enjoyed it.

Together we went into the living room. I lit some candles and turned on our fairy lights. The room was dominated by the huge birth pool, finally in place and functioning after a week of leaks and hassle. The room was warm, comforting, like a calm womb itself. Above the pool, in silver, the phases of the moon were depicted; on the opposite wall, a large golden sun. This space would be our alchemical laboratory, our magickal birth chamber. Pink flowers and images of Yemanja (the Orisha goddess of motherhood and the ocean) and the great bear (Helen and I had been working with the image of the Bear Mother to help her 'bear' the pain of labour) were present.

I lit an aromatherapy burner of suitable oils and put on, at Helens behest some dub music. To the sounds of Lee 'Scratch' Perry we danced together, Helen holding onto me each time a contraction hit, leaning against me and pulling on my body. Between each wave she belly-danced, imagining a rope of light falling from between her legs, spiralling as she danced upon the floor, coiling onto the ground, taking the pain and the baby with it. As the uterus contracts it spirals up, eventually as the child emerges it spirals through mother's pelvis. The spiral had been a key symbol for Helen during her pregnancy.

The doorbell sounded and I left Helen's side for a moment to answer it. In came Vanessa, the midwife. She bundled in her equipment. Cylinders of nitrous oxide, bags containing pads, needles and aspirating equipment.

'I'd like to give you an internal examination Helen if that's ok', she asked gently.

Helen agreed and lay down on the daybed. It was obvious that this position made the pain of each contraction much harder to bear. I recall thinking about all those poor women who, through the whim of a French King, had to labour in this insane posture.

Between contractions Vanessa inserted her fingers. 'That's really good Helen, tell me to stop at any time, there's no problem…ok, I can feel your babies head. That's one of the great honours of my job is that I get to feel the baby first. He's still got a way to go but you're doing great, you're about 4 centimetres dilated."

Vanessa withdrew her hand and checked Osric's heartbeat. There it was, clear as a bell, the whoosh, whoosh, whoosh of about 140 beats per minute, strong and well.

"Look, if you're doing ok, I'll just go next door and wait for you to call me" said Vanessa. She made me a cup of tea (Helen was taking regular sips of water by this point), took advantage of the gardening section of our library and went to sit in the bedroom.

Helen and I kept dancing.

I was watching the clock, the red digits shining fixed and angry looking. I was timing each contraction, timing the period between them and conscious of the overall time the labour was taking. Like tripping, ages would pass, with deep contractions getting stronger and stronger. I put on a tape of Middle Eastern belly dancing music as Helen clung to me more intensely. I was rubbing Helen's body with perfumed oils, talking constantly, slow and low. Between contractions Helen sat, resting, trying to save her energy.

"Breath easily, let your jaw loosen, relax and let your body do it, you are doing it, you can do this, you're beautiful, you're wonderful, I love you, your body knows exactly what to do, let each wave pass through you, I love you, you can do this, your baby is coming Helen, you can do it, I love you, you are amazing…' words wrapped round and round like a spiral of text, clothing and soothing.

Vanessa came back in at about 4 o'clock and checked Osric's heart rate again and gave Helen another examination, 7cms dilated and baby's heart rate vigorous and regular as ever. Vanessa watched me supporting

Helen, she helped wonderfully, rubbing Helens back and saying "mmmmm, you're doing really well Helen, mmmmm, you're amazing". I continued to feed Helen sips of water and homeopathic aconite, to help her with fear.

Then it became much harder.

I recall Helen bending over the work surface in the kitchen. Her dressed only in a T-shirt, me in shorts (ready to go into the pool). I remember rubbing her back as she bent over, pressing her arms hard into the white melamine. She was crying.

"It really hurts, it really hurts! I can't do it! It really hurts!"

I kept my cycle of reassurance going, trying to smile rather than get entangled in the horror of seeing the person I love in such agony. Reassuring. 'You can do it, relax and breathe, breathe through each contraction'.

I could see them hitting her, forcing her body forward like a swimmer hit by a wave on the shore. Bending under the weight, the power of each contraction. Helen wept," I can't!"

And suddenly my lover was five years old, a scared and hurt child, unable to fight off this hateful thing, this cruel process. I remained strong, calling upon the power that I had filled myself up with over the preceding months. The Ori, the Hawk Headed god Horus. These powers, the yellow solar energy of the Holy Guardian Angel, the defending, potent force of the Martian current. I deployed these things as strength, as gentle power. I remembered what Helen's yoga teacher had said on the partner's yoga session.

"The woman's job is to let go, the partner's job is to hold the faith. To defend the labouring woman from unwelcome intervention and to defend and uphold the fact that she can do this, she can give birth to her baby."

Helen indicated that she wanted me to stop rubbing her back as she was bent over. I recall thinking that this, combined with her reaching a low ebb meant that she was beginning transition. She was moving from the first stage of labour to the beginning of the second expulsive stage. I gave Helen homeopathic gelsemium, a remedy recommended at this point.

Vanessa was in the room with us, and we suggested to Helen that she might want to try the pool. She got into the warm water, gingerly stepping over the wall of the structure between contractions.

"I can't do this, it hurts!" said Helen.

"Oh Helen, you're doing wonderfully!" said Vanessa, "you could be in an advert for natural childbirth! You're doing great!"

Helen got into the pool and bent over the edge, gripping the walls and crying out. I got in beside her, holding her hand in mine.

Whether it was the warmth of the pool or whether it was simply the passage of the labour, but that was when the process stepped up a gear. Now Helen was really crying out. Between contractions she breathed short, stabbing exhalations. As each wave hit she was forced deeper into a disconnected, trance like state.

"Well, I think I'd like to call the second midwife, Helen, because I think that baby is coming pretty soon!" explained Vanessa. I was also aware that Vanessa's shift would soon be ending, and unless Osric was born soon she might have to go.

I watched the clock, it was getting towards eight o'clock. Helen had been in established labour for about eight hours. My mind mulled over friends who had shorter labours, I didn't dare think about the horror stories of other friends; 29 hours, 36 hours, longer.

Vanessa let in the second midwife, an older woman called Jill. At first my hackles were raised. This was change, a new person entering this already established drama. Jill also seemed a little brusquer than Vanessa, perhaps she was more 'old school' and would be less tolerant of our hippie ideas.

I was in the pool beside Helen, Jill was in front of Helen who clung to the edge of the pool, pressing down with all her might as each contraction hit.

"Get away!"

Inwardly I summoned all the energy I had, all the power, all the gods and prayed with all my heart and mind. Let it happen, let Osric come, let him come, let him come out!

"Okay, Helen", said Jill "I'd like to try you in a standing squat, I think it will help get that baby out".

I stood, arms held outward, Helen resting her arms over mine. Then as each contraction hit she would let go, letting the weight of her body transfer to my arms, pushing down and out.

"That's it, Helen, that's very good," said Jill, her voice firm and authoritative, "just push that baby out, like a big shit, push it out".

For a moment I was uncertain, weren't we supposed to let the baby come out, to breath it out gently, not push it out like a turd?

I felt Helen drop onto my arms, my muscles straining to hold her weight which was greater than my own.

"Go on Helen push that baby out." Jill bent down in front of Helen "that's it! that's right!"

I tensed my arms, calling on the Great Bear Mother to help me, to make me strong enough to bear Helen's labouring body.

"Okay, Helen now squat down." asked Jill.

I sat in a chair and held my arms out again, this time between contractions. Helen sat on a little stool that had been supplied with the birth pool.

"Ah, ah, ah!" Helen cried, a very different sound from the long and deep moaning of labour, "that really hurts!". She was out of the deep trance, her voice back to it's usual modulation. What hurt was the stretching of her yoni.

"Don't let me tear!" she asked Jill. Meanwhile Jill had phoned for the second midwife as the baby was due to arrive very soon, and she had also found a mirror (in fact the magick mirror that I'd used for a number of Ori rituals).

"Would you like to see the baby crowning?" asked Jill. She held the mirror beneath Helen and, the ultrasound scan notwithstanding, for the first time I could see my son!

"Okay, who's going to catch this baby?" asked Jill.

Then, in one powerful contraction, Osric was born. Helen gathered him up in her arms and Jill hastily wrapped a warmed towel round his body. In the strange light of sunshine filtering through our blue curtains, with Jill holding a triple candlestick (in the shape of a letter Shin) beside us, Osric wailed. His tiny arms open and wide, his skin appearing strangely blue in the light, his head distinctly hairy, with little ringlets plastered in blood and vermix. I recall reaching round Helen and wrapping my arms about her and our baby.

"Okay, the cord has already stopped pumping; was it you, Helen, who's going to cut it?" Jill asked in a clear, calm voice.

According to our birth plan, Helen was going to cut the cord after it had stopped pumping blood (and the last drops of energy) into Osric.

"Jules can do it" she said, her arms full with the still screaming bundle.

I reached down below Helen and took the scissors that Jill handed me. The cord had been sealed with plastic clips and was pale white, like a telephone cable. With some difficulty, the scissors not being very sharp, I cut through it.

The moments that followed are dizzy in my mind. Where Osric had been born was just to one side of our birth pool. Carpet tiles I'd placed around the pool were covered in blood. I took Osric to hold against my skin, he had stopped yelling and the grey colour of his hands and feet was beginning to be replaced with a healthier looking pink.

The doorbell sounded and the third midwife came in, a younger woman who set about helping Helen onto an incontinence pad on our daybed.

I moved to sit beside her, with Osric still whimpering in my arms. A photo was taken. Then Osric was passed to Helen to feed. I had already felt him try to latch on to my abdomen and so it was quite clear that his suck reflex was fine.

As Helen held him to her breast and the third midwife helped her I could see the expression of pain on her face as Osric began to suckle. I clearly sympathised with Helen's pain, felt it wrench at my gut, after all that work, all that labour, the pain still wasn't over. I found and gave Helen homeopathic arnica to treat her bruising.

Our female cat 'Lam' had been hovering around. Despite all the fuss, the doorbell and the number of people she seemed drawn to be beside Helen. Jill asked if Helen could push her placenta out but Helen simply didn't have enough energy to do it, so with an injection it was delivered, a large slab of meat, later to be buried in our garden.

The third midwife busied herself making us some tea, and both Jill and the third midwife examined Helen, explaining that there were two small tears around her yoni. Stitches were sewn which, even with a local anaesthetic, was still a very painful process.

I remember then holding my son in my arms, somewhat quieter after his first feed, and watching Helen, her back and legs streaked with blood, crawling towards the bathroom.

"…I told her I didn't and crawled off to wee in the bath" quipped Helen, misquoting the Beatles *Norwegian Wood*. Helen bathed and I went to sit beside her, holding Osric tight, wrapped again in his towel.

Both midwives busied themselves tidying up the flat, scrubbing away blood from the carpet and throws, disposing of used gloves, pads and so on.

After her bath we returned to the living room. The third midwife fitted Osric's first nappy and he was dressed in a white baby grow. The candled gutted and went out, it was by now about 2pm. We thanked the midwives and they left. Once more we were alone, except that we would never be two people alone again. Now we were three.

We lay in our bed with Osric between us. Knowing that all was well I immediately slept. Helen only dozed watching the little human who now nestled beside her.

Beside the window in our living room I had pinned up three paintings. Helen had painted one during each trimester of her pregnancy. The first showed two stylised figures, her and me, with her body swollen and pregnant, and me holding her in my arms. The second was the figure of a bulls head, painted at about the same time that I had undertaken a Mithras ritual (organised by a member of the PACT magickal group) where the energy I had raised I had dedicated to protecting my family. The third image showed Helen and I in a boat on a deep green sea. Around the edge was written 'Please don't fall overboard – don't become like Maneros'. Maneros was the child of Queen Astarte. His name means 'understanding of love'. According to myth, Maneros travelled in a barge that bore away the tree trunk coffin in which the dead Osiris lay. When Isis opened the coffin and threw herself upon the body of her dead husband Maneros was overwhelmed by the sight of the goddess' love. He swooned and 'because of the awe of her' died and fell overboard.

I have always been amazed, transfixed by childbirth. The power of it, the intense reality and meaning of that single event. When I've seen films that contained scenes of birth I've pretty much always wept. In her painting Helen was asking me to be strong for her labour, not to be swept away in awe by the power of the goddess, but to be able to be a competent birth companion.

Part of what had helped me to achieve this was the intense period of magickal work that had preceded and run parallel with Helen's Pregnancy. First the Ori, the Holy Guardian Angel (HGA) work which was focused around Tiphereth. It was while I was working with this sephira that I discovered that I was literally to have a son (sun). Since the HGA is, in one sense, 'the Other', Osric represents and is the physical expression of my HGA. He is that which takes me beyond myself, stops me becoming a cynical and selfish 30 something. He is a being that I adore and love, who is from me, with me, and yet is totally as Crowley puts it, 'Thou who art I, beyond all I am'.

With the PACT group we had done a Ma'at ritual, which on a personal level had allowed me to move from the Tiphereth sphere to begin to enter the realm of Geburah (and perhaps conjured the cool and calm Jill, who I later discovered is well known as one of the most experienced midwives in the town).

My final major ritual before the labour was, in part, aimed at helping me to maintain my focus and strength throughout the bloody, Martian process of birth (our culture identified Mars as the god of blood shed in warfare, but this blood can also be the blood shed in birth). The ritual I organised was an invocation of Ra-Hoor-Khuit the hawk headed god.

Later, as the birth gifts for Osric arrived my Thelemic friends brought him gold and frankincense (emblematic of Tiphereth), and my friend the Professor sent him a miniature Horus hawk. Whether or not the Professor recalled the fact that he had given a similar one to me for my 30th birthday (a somewhat larger image) I'm not sure. In his note that attended the gift he said that he'd thought of a hawk 'since Osric shares 3 of the five letters of this name with Horus'. Osric, I now realise, contains the word 'Ori' within it also.

So in terms of my own spiritual unfolding (which I have been recently framing within Qabalistic terms) labour represented an exploration of Geburah and in some ways, Atu XI Strength or Lust. The paradox of labour is the same as the one depicted in the traditional image of Strength: that to ride or control the lion woman must use gentle 'active passivity'. The image is explicitly that of Babalon the Whore who gives herself up to 'all men', the chalice into which the magickian seeks to pour every last droplet of blood. Birth relies on giving up, on letting your body do the work – the lesson is that of letting go and permitting the process to happen through you. For the birth partner, the lesson was that to help, I needed to maintain a gentle strength. A slow burning Leonine flame of presence and support, I needed to be strong so that I wasn't tipped into the abyss like Maneros.

If we permit ourselves to consider the De Leon/Simeon bar Yochai ie 'classic western' glyph as a topographic as well as conceptual map. The path of the Lion headed serpent (Teth) on the tree also lies beside the Veil of the Abyss. During labour Helen was fairly unaware of (though by no means unaffected by) my mantra of support or indeed of much that

---

* Later Helen painted a fourth painting in her sequence. A image of this abyss. She captioned it with an quote from a Siberian shaman "The only true wisdom lives far from humans, out in the great loneliness, and it can be reached only through suffering."

was going on around her. Certainly, her sense of time was dramatically altered. That Helen found herself in a markedly altered state of consciousness is unsurprising. But what is particularly interesting is that, at one stage Helen found herself in a place. The place had an explicit reality of the type that DMT can conjure. She found herself standing alone on a silent, featureless and flat plane. The whole environment was monochrome and still. Beside her she could see a huge abyss. In talks with other women who have experienced labour it turns out that this vision of an abyss on a plane maybe a common experience that attends labour.*

And now what? Well, the journey continues. Daily there are the devotions to the son of the Sun - my fabulous baby (nappies must be changed morning, midday, dusk and midnight at the very least!). This is a devotional yoga that daily is repaid with smiles and the privilege of watching the dawning of a new human intelligence. Helen is seated as The Empress on her nursing chair, offering her life to Osric so he may grow.

When she is ready she intends to have a red lotus signed with the mantra 'Krim' tattooed on her lower back, marking her dedication of her labour to Ma Kali.

For me the journey towards Chesed, the sephira of the Father. The challenge to understand fatherhood as something better than the old Jehovah patriarch ('dry desert god with no sense of humour' as the band James put it).

Peter Carroll, writing about parenthood in *Psybermagick*, calls it a way of 'throwing bombs at the future'. Well, explosives have always been Pete's style. I rather prefer the gardening metaphor myself. In raising my son, I am raising myself. By having children I have become part of something greater, my ego-self merely a spoke on the wheel of life. Thus there is no apocalypse anymore, no end of history, for I shall die daily and be reborn with each new growing wave of consciousness, with each new being that comes into the world. How to meet this challenge? Well, gently. Like Jean Parvati says, you can do parenthood as hassle or parenthood as meditation. Just listen to the sound of your breathing and relax, everything else will happen in good time...

When a woman has a baby it is a more powerful moment than a death. For in death there is only the ending of the animation of the body and the initiation of gradual process of decay. In birth the mother creates both a life and therefore a death. This is the Kali puja, the great mystery of time and of the cycles within the Tao.

Wait, I hear my baby calling, time to end this ramble and begin my new life.

The use of the imagination

"the literal is the enemy"

James Hillman

"the imagination is the root of human reality."

Marc Fonda

The faculty we know as imagination is the fundamental process whereby we structure our world. It is the facility of human consciousness that allows us to model the universe inside our own heads and then to project this outward, reinterpreting the experience as sense data.

For example, when you look with your eyes upon the world you perceive the world 'out there'. Although we know that the light hitting the receptive cells of the eye, generating an electro-chemical interaction within the brain is the basis of seeing, for this event to have any use and any meaning (as a perception of the outside world) it must be broadcast outward into the world. The screen upon which we project our perceptions is imagination; it is the necessary condition of experience.

Imagination is the basis of social interaction. As well as creating my world I come to create an interpenetrating world that is yours. I know that the contents of your mind are similar and yet different to mine, I may know that I know something that you cannot. Without this understanding, I am autistic, unable to develop a full theory of mind, limited in my empathy.

We know that our imagination, or perception of the world, can be easily altered, even manipulated. We are all aware of not seeing the wood for the trees, of hallucinations, misperceptions and of being tricked. With this in mind we may seek to transcend our imagined world, to invent systems of action that seek to know the Real World, shorn of the fallibility of perception. Through experimental science we have tried to do this, through the production of the laboratory. This approach yields many interesting results, the reliability of which is a testament to the remarkable interpenetration of our subjective realities. However, the very act of making scientific models is predicated on the imaginative substrate that experimentation seeks to get around. Moreover, as

71

magickian enchants for wealth and a neighbour becomes rich the operation has been a success.

By actively engaging with the 'images' in the imaginal realm, by treating them as real in their own terms (seeing gods as gods and not neurological events nor psychologised complexes) the occultist cultivates an enchanted soul. The body is renewed, the heart no longer only a hydraulic pump but the location of imagination, joy and love. The purpose of life becomes an exponentially increasing rapture in experience. Every moment in perception becomes charged with meaning and power, and equally each form is seen as being but a transient stance of perception which, as Spare puts it, 'Does not matter, need not be'.

The 'loss' of the Golden Age can be discovered by this method not to be a longing for the past but a desire for the future. The desire for the 'good old days' is the baulked project of our inherent epistemaphillia of which the communitas of the intra-uterine existence is only a staging post. By engaging fully with imagination we are putting ourselves fully into relationship with the world, and by doing so we are recuperating the Amina Mundi. Thus the Great Work undoes The Fall, instead casting an enchantment of emerging possibility and richness. Through this process Kether is married to Malkuth, God becomes aware of itself and Taoist immortality becomes natural and complete.

Drugs and the Qabalah

The principle of correspondence forms a central element in the use and structure of the Qabalah. In correspondence we can observe the idea that all the universe is interconnected and that connection can be seen as shifting patterns of meaning, both rational and poetic. Think of a classic chain of correspondence:

Geburah=Mars=red=iron=blood=wrath=ruby=pepper=Horus=5=the ritual scourge

...and so on.

Within the chains, or perhaps webs, of correspondence many different modes of experience are linked. So sight (red) is linked to smell (pepper) and to inner emotional states (wrath). In this way the model of the universe which correspondence systems build up is a truly holistic one, involving many different types of experience. Systems such as the Qabalah represent frameworks upon which the principle of correspondence can be hung. Thus the principle is that 'all things are interconnected' or 'as above, so below' and the key images around which these webs of correspondence are spun are the sephira. The system of correspondences is like a circle in that we can measure it beginning anywhere. By this I mean that the Qabalist will start with the framework principle of Sephiroth and build out from there the web of correspondence shown above. People who favour the runes will use the runic letters as their framework and work out from there.

Just as the consideration of correspondences for 'animals, real and imaginary' provides useful information (eg imagery for pathworkings, rituals, analysis of dreams etc), so does the classification of drugs. Crowley, that arch drug fiend and Qabalist, sought to relate drugs to his understanding of the Qabalah. Here is an example of one scheme he developed:

Sephira	Vegetable drug
Kether	Elixir Vitae
Chockmah	Hashish

75

Binah	Belladonna
Chesed	Opium
Geburah	Tobacco
Tiphereth	Alcohol
Netzach	Damiana
Hod	Mescaline
Yesod	Orchid root
Malkuth	Corn

What Crowley is doing here is very much within the tradition of correspondence. He is seeking to link abstract metaphysical concepts (Chesed) with the embodied, subjective experience of a drug (opium). He is also relating the physical activity of the drug to abstract qualities. For example he relates Tiphereth to alcohol but also to digitalis and coffee, presumably because both drugs stimulate the heart, and Tiphereth is of course the heart of the Qabalah.

For Crowley the use of drugs was a legitimate means of self-exploration. Whilst I would certainly acknowledge that drug use does have its pitfalls, I would agree with The Beast that these materials can be used as sacramental substances as part of esoteric work. There is the problem of the illegality of certain substances in some countries but that is a different (though, of course related) issue which I don't address here

The effect of different drugs, just like the effect of different styles of music, can be tremendously variable. Different people, depending on their physiology, mental state, environment and many other factors can have very different reactions to the same drug. Moreover the reactions of a given individual can also vary across time, sometimes quite dramatically. Having said that most people who have more than a passing familiarity with a given drug will begin to get a sense of the character of the drug as it relates to them. For some people they may find that the drug just does not like them (for instance, you may like the taste and the warming drunkenness to be found in red wine but discover that it always gives you a crushing hangover the next day).

For some people exploration of different drug states may give them an appreciation of the different moods, likes and dislikes of the 'spirit' of the drug. In this way, over time and through different experiments the individual can begin to build up their own Qabalah of drug experience.

Sephira	Drug
Kether	Ayahuasca
Chockmah	LSD
Binah	Ketamine
Chesed	Cocaine
Geburah	Amphetamine
Tiphereth	Ecstasy
Netzach	Salvia Divinorum
Hod	Psilocybin
Yesod	2-CB
Malkuth	Chocolate

In this way they can further extend the range and depth of the correspondence system to include drug materials. In fact if we stop to consider for a moment what exactly a drug is, we can see that these correspondences are not much different from many others. For example the colour red is an external stimulus which is processed by the brain (ie becomes an electro-chemical event) and is contextualised by a range of personal and social factors (eg 'I like red', 'red means stop', etc). A drug is a physical material which, introduced into the body works in the same way. The reaction of the drug to the individual organism becomes an electro-chemical event which is then contextualised by one's own feelings and those of the culture surrounding one (eg 'ecstasy makes me feel happy', 'The Papers tell me ecstasy is dangerous', etc).

Of course, the different moods of one particular drug spirit might also be plotted through correspondence using the Qabalah as our framework. For instance:

Sephira	Cannabis, forms of use.
Kether	As an aid to meditation
Chockmah	Used to enhance ritual work
Binah	Hashish consumed orally (soporific)
Chesed	Used as a compliment to other drugs (eg MDMA, Cocaine)
Geburah	With tobacco
Tiphereth	'The giggles'
Netzach	Home-grown, an aphrodisiac
Hod	As a confuser, storyteller
Yesod	Bringer of dreams
Malkuth	As a drug that makes you feel hungry, 'the munchies'

A quick glance around the globe shows that many spiritual traditions make significant use of drugs to change consciousness and attain what some call 'gnosis'. From the highly developed shamanic cultures of the Americas (where novel and potent brews of psychedelic plants, such as those contained in the ayahuasca preparation, hail from), through to the use of cannabis by the Indian Sadhu. In the western world, whilst there are some limited accounts of drugs being used within the occult tradition, our knowledge and literature on the subject is only now being rediscovered and developed. Although there is some 'outlaw tradition' of the use of herbs such as aconite, belladonna and henbane recorded in witchcraft trials, the repertoire of psychedelic knowledge in the west is tremendously impoverished. For instance in north western Europe, psychedelic mushrooms are native and are an ideal naturally occurring sacred sacrament. Yet, despite such mushrooms being a key element in New World shamanism, there is no record of them being used in Europe for ritual practice until the 1950s!

Interestingly as Crowley (and many of his colleagues including Mather and Allan Bennett) helped reclaim and maintain the tradition of using drugs in western occultism, as a Qabalist, he simultaneously reminds us of our shamanic roots. Like the shaman of Siberia who climbs through the levels of reality while high on psychedelic mushrooms, so Crowley bids us ascend the tree of life with drugs as potential allies in the spiritual quest.

As the practical use of esoteric systems as the Qabalah develop, so a relationship between the use of drugs and other techniques of the system may appear. For example, drugs that promote lucid dreaming and hypnagogic imagery might be combined with techniques such as pathworking. Drugs may be found that enhance physical ritual or trance dance also.

The increasing distribution of knowledge about traditional drug preparations (such as peyote, ayahuasca or ibogaine) as well as new laboratory creations (such as 2-CB or MDMA) provides us with an ever increasing range of pharmacological allies for one's own inner journey. Just as Crowley discovered that yogic meditative practices blended spectacularly with hashish (Crowley's first experience of the peak state of Samadhi was allied to his use of cannabis) so each occultist can discover which practices blend well with what drugs. Of course this is not to suggest that the magickian must use all or indeed any drugs. Drugs are part of the toolkit of spiritual exploration, no different in their value from learning the art of sitting still and observing the breath, or of visualisation.

I believe that the time is right for us to re-discover the value of drugs as a means of altering consciousness and of exploring ourselves. Many substances that are now available provide excellent tools with which we can explore our own minds and our relationship with the rest of the universe. Certainly it would be a mistake to assume that all drug experience is valuable or 'true' (though the same can be said of dreams or insights from divination) but that is no reason to throw the baby out with the bath-water.

Further reading
Food of the Gods – Terence McKenna, 1992
Pharmakon – Julian Vayne, 2001

PIHKAL – Alexander & Ann Shulgin, 1991

Plants of the Gods – Albert Hofmann, Richard Evans Schultes, 1979

Psychedelics Encyclopedia – Peter Stafford, 1991

The Doors of Perception – Aldous Huxley, 1954

The Essential Psychedelic Guide – DM.Turner, 1994

Useful websites

www.ecstasy.org

www.erowid.org

www.liminalspace.co.uk

www.lycaeum.org

www.transform-drugs.org.uk

Two Worlds and In-between:
The changing concepts and use of space in modern magick

(A paper given at an academic conference on the subject of magick at University of Bristol.)

In this paper I will examine trends in the magical use of space. I will specifically be examining those spaces that are peculiar to ritual or ceremonial activity and suggesting some ways that these spaces can be seen to have changed in the last 100 years or so. Such spaces are variously referred to as temples, zones of sacred space, magic circles and by many other names. These are areas where the physical dimensions of height, depth and breadth touch the esoteric conception of the world and give rise to more or less delineated locations which are the theatres or laboratories within which magical praxis takes place.

In order to explore these areas I will be concentrating on examples drawn directly from modern English language esoteric writing. Moreover, I wish to explore the development of modern magical interpretations of space primarily through the words of sorcerers themselves rather than through secondary interpretative texts.

Perhaps one of the most significant grimoires in the development of modern occultism is the *Book of the Sacred Magic of Abramelin the Mage*, translated by one-time head of the Hermetic Order of the Golden Dawn S.L. MacGregor Mathers and published in 1898. The text documents a lengthy meditative and devotional practice which, if undertaken with sufficient zeal, leads to 'Knowledge and Conversation' with one's Holy Guardian Angel. Such a meeting with what contemporary occultists often describe as one's higher self, genius or True Will, is necessary, according to the Abramelin grimoire, in order to be sufficiently pure of mind and spirit to be able to handle the demons which the later section of the book deals with. These demons are capable of any number of marvellous feats, such as allowing the magicians to cause food to miraculously appear, to discover hidden treasures or inflame passion between any two persons.

attacked Neuburg in the form of a 'naked savage' but Neuburg was able to repel the spirit with divine names and his magickal dagger. Once Choronzon retreated to the triangle the circle was repaired by Neuburg.

So, again we see a direct correspondence between the physical delineation of space and the occult virtues it possesses. The literal circle is identical with the symbolic protective space. However, as we move toward the present we can see that this literal interpretation on magical space begins, in many thought not all cases, to be supplanted by a more flexible approach.

A key text which is very much in use today is *Liber Null*, first published in 1978. This book played a vital part in galvanising the emergence of the Chaos Magic school of occultism. Author Pete Carroll does not provide a practice for the construction of the magic circle per se, rather his emphasis is on developing an effective Banishing ritual:

> "A well-constructed banishing ritual has the following effects. It prepares the magician more rapidly for magical concentration than any of the trance exercises alone. It enables the magician to resist obsession if problems are encountered with dream experiences or sigils becoming conscious. It also protects the magician from any hostile occult influences which may assail him."

He goes on:

> "First, the magician describes a barrier about himself with the magical weapon. The barrier is also strongly visualised. Three dimensional figures are preferable."

In the text, illustrations depict the magician standing within a sphere or pyramid.

For contemporary chaos magicians, banishing rituals are not predominately used to banish malignant forces outside of the sorcerer's self as much as they are about banishing the internal dialogue that would detract the magician from attaining a suitably focused state of mind to deploy occult power.

The boundary of the banished space is nowhere near as clear as it is in the Goetia. What we are seeing here is an increasing tendency to locate the boundary of the circle not in physical space (such as chalk marks on the floor) but in an *imaginal* space. Henry Corbin coined the term imaginal to distinguish the creative form of imagination which "has notic value...it is an organ of knowledge because it 'creates' being". This ontologically positive depiction of imagination is a valuable tool when we come to examine contemporary magical practice.

We can clearly see this change from the primary location of the circle's boundary from the physical to imaginal realm within the praxis of many contemporary occult groups. A circle may be cast within a square room and the boundary of the circle is imagined to include the whole floor area of the chamber. Although the edges of the circle may (theoretically) extend into the room adjacent this does not mean that ones neighbours are inadvertent participants in your ceremony! Rather, the circle exists in an imaginal space and though an actual perimeter may be described (with either a wand or chalk) this is essentially a secondary representation, the primary reality of the circle is non-physical. Doreen Valientie, one of the founding figures of Wicca, emphasises in *Witchcraft for Tomorrow* that:

> "It is your effort and visualisation that make a magic circle, not material things like twine or [lines drawn on] carpet".

Alongside the shift of focus from a literal to an imaginal circle or magical space there is also a shift of emphasis in terms of the role of the magical space itself. Rather than being primarily defensive, for many modern practitioners, the magickal space exists as a theatre in which esoteric powers interact. The inside of the circle becomes a sacred space, suffused with the divine essences of the pagan gods who are conjured into it. The American witch Starhawk in her book *Truth or Dare* explains:

> "Witches traditionally "cast a circle". We draw a circle, usually with a wand or knife, visualising an energy boundary taking form. I generally see it in my mind as a barrier of blue flame."

So here the idea of the circle as a 'barrier' is still explicit.

She continues:

"The circle contains the energy that we raise, so that it can stay focused and reach a greater intensity."

For Starhawk the exact location of the circle is of less importance than the intensity and intention with which it is drawn. She describes it as "touching each of the walls and corners". As with the praxis of chaos magic, the initial act of creating this sacred space is that of banishing any influences that might hinder the operation:

"Then we say something like: 'This circle has become a free space. All the voices, telling us what we can't do or be, what we should think or say, telling us we're bad or wrong or stupid or crazy - leave right now! In this circle we are each the Goddess, the God, the open channel for the moving energies of life...Now, all you energies we don't need or want, be gone!'"

So in Starhawk's description of the magic circle we see this area as being about the concentration of magical power, rather than defence against demons. Paul Huson, in his book *Mastering Witchcraft*, nicely summarises the differences of approach:

"To those familiar with Cabalistic sorcery, the magic circle is generally viewed as a means of defence against hostile spirit entities; to the witch, however, though it may serve this purpose in some of her spells, it has a far more important function usually. This is, in fact, to serve as a lens to focus the witch power that she raises in her rituals. It is a sort of magical boiler tank in which the steam is compressed in order to channel it into some useful activity such as driving a piston rod."

However, as an examination of other contemporary occult groups shows, the perceived changes in the role of the magic circle cannot be neatly divided into ceremonial magic vs. witchcraft. Rather, in most contemporary occult texts there is a general move away from the confrontational style of demonic evocation in the *Sacred Magic* and *Goetia*. This change in the relationships in magical space reflects deeper ontological changes in the approach to the occult powers the magician seeks to contact. These forces are no longer so 'outside', so 'other'. The occult universe seems to have become gradually less hostile than it was in Crowley's day, with an understandable increase in the use of self transformative, psychological interpretations of magic.

The physical, literal circle gives way to a circle that is located more substantially in the imaginal than the physical realm. This new circle, or occult space, is closer to a laboratory or theatre than it is to a defensive palisade, it is a space where the usual rules of reality may be suspended, where the gods walk and where magick reigns.

More recently magical space has been re-imagined as an area in which normal Law or perhaps the hegemony of the modern State can be suspended. Hakim Bey (a writer that has greatly influenced the modern chaos school of magic) describes such areas in his influential work *The Temporary Autonomous Zone, Ontological Anarchy, Poetic Terrorism*

"Sorcery works at creating around itself a psychic/physical space or openings into a space of untrammelled expression"

He goes on to explore the location and form of such spaces:

"I believe that by extrapolating from past and future stories about "islands in the net" we may collect evidence to suggest that a certain kind of "free enclave" is not only possible in our time but also existent. All my research and speculation has crystallized around the concept of the TEMPORARY AUTONOMOUS ZONE (hereafter abbreviated TAZ)."

Such a free space provides the base camp from which the guerrilla ontological tactics that Bey espouses can be practised. His marriage of revolutionary politics and occultism informs a wide variety of modern esoteric traditions. The shifting, changing, fluid nature of the TAZ allows Bey to propose the existence of such spaces within existing information nets (of which the internet is a perfect example). It should therefore not surprise us to find 'virtual rituals' taking place in cyberspace. Practitioners of such rituals include the z(cluster) which describes its origins as:

"...founded in New Orleans in 1995 in a churlish fit of resentment against magickal orders by Marik and FireClown. Sodden with the ideology of Hakim Bey, outraged by the so called "hierarchical gambit" of Pete Carroll and devoted to the freelance shamanism of Jan Fries, the impoverished but innovative duo decided to create a wholly incomprehensible (but practical) disorganization."

The virtual TAZ is the situation for experiments in what z(cluster) term 'magickal terrorism', that is "an assault on normative belief patterns, an attack on the mind's status quo, guerrilla war on the careful considerations of consciousness." A document published by Marik on the z(clutser) site explains:

"Those who are interested in the practice of Chaos Magick are warned that Chaos Magick can be, well, chaotic. Since it is designed to deconstruct belief, dearly held opinions, the stories we tell ourselves to lull ourselves into a sense of security will tend to fray and unravel. Unless the magician is willing to forsake these old ideas, to allow the boundaries of personal identity to be disrupted the result of magickal action may be chaotic indeed. Dramatic life changes, sometimes perceived as being for the worse, are a commonly reported result of Chaos Magickal Rites. Fundamentally, Chaos Magick is not about discovering one's True Will, nor communing with the Mother Goddess, nor even associating with demons, but with the direct, startling apprehension of the Chaos current, the quantum flux of an unhuman universe. Chaos Magick is magickal terrorism."

Another magickal organisation that has much in common with the z(cluster), Thee Temple Ov Psychick Youth refer to one form of their magical space as 'Thee Nursery'. Thee Nursery is a location in which we can regress to our primary impulses. Through ritual, trance, sex, drug use and other practices we can de-construct or de-condition ourselves in preparation for emerging as something 'rich and strange'. The magickal space for TOPYites is a space in which a radical self-transformation takes place.

So the circle, for some occultists, is no longer the place of safety from demons as much as it is a location for a radical, perhaps dangerous, self-transformative project.

By conceptualising magic as primarily an self-transformative process, driven by the imagination, we are adopting a model of magical action which Frater UD terms the 'psychological model'. Frater UD (a German magician and former member of the Chaos Magic Order the Illuminates of Thanateros) details a series of five models of magic in his seminal essay *Models of Magic* - briefly these are: the spirit model, the energy model, the psychological model, the information model, and the meta-model. Within the psychological model of magic:

> "The psychological model of magic does not purport to explain how magic works, its only premise is that the subconscious (or, as Carl Jung later retagged it, the unconscious) will do the job if it is properly addressed and/or conditioned. This again is achieved by magical trance, suggestion and the use of symbols (i.e. selective sensory input) as tools of association and as a means of communication between the magician's conscious will and his subconscious faculty responsible for putting it into effect. "

Although modern magicians continue to use what on the surface we might consider to be the spirit model (calling upon demons, gods, elemental beings and such) the observations I have made concerning the changes in magical space challenge such a view. As the physical boundary or other elements in the magickal space have become re-located into the imaginal realm, so have our spirits. Today the demons dwell within us more than they do in the triangle.

Bey, Hakim, 1985, 1991 T. A. Z.- The Temporary Autonomous Zone, Ontological Anarchy, Poetic Terrorism Autonomedia Anti-copyright

http://www.hermetic.com/bey/taz_cont.html

Corbin, Henry 1969 Creative Imagination in Sufism of Ibn'Arabi trans Ralph Manheim Princeton University Press

Crowley, Aleister 1973 (Originally published privately 1912 as Book 4 Part II) Magick   RKP

Crowley, Aleister 1998 (reprinted) The Vision and the Voice With Commentary and Other Papers Vol 4 Red Wheel/Weiser

Frater U.'.D.'. 1991   Models of Magic www.chaosmatrix.org/library/chaos/texts/model.html

Huson, Paul   1970   Mastering Witchcraft Rupert Hert-Davis

Marik 1995   Chaos Magick: Magickal Terrorism http://members.aol.com/zcluster/Pages/magterr.html

Mathers, SL (Trans.)   1976   Book Of The Sacred Magic Of Abramelin The Mage Dover Publications http://w3.one.net/~browe/pdf/abramelin_book3.pdf

Rapoza, J. A. (Ed.)   1994   Thee Psychick bible : thee apocryphal scriptures ov Genesis P-Orridge & thee third mind of psychic TV Alecto Enterprises

Starhawk 1990 Truth or Dare Harper and Row

Valientie Doreen 1978 Witchcraft for tomorrow Hale

Wetzel, Joshua S 2001 The Paradigmal Pirate (Liber LLL & Liber Ventum) Privately published

The Rite of the South Western Arrow

(An Invocation of Pomba Gira de las Siete Encrsliadas.)

This is a ritual that had evolved over time. With no single statement of Will, perhaps no clear intention, certainly no clearer than any answer one might get from questions such as "Why did you paint that painting Mr Artist?" or "why did you bother evolving the sea horse Mother Nature?"

A collage of images leading to this rite: my arrival in Bideford, once a great port now a tiny town on the banks of the river Torridge: my work with the Ori[1], my first working with Pomba Gira in Brighton led by Frater Kondwani, my seeing Pomba Gira (resplendent in wide brimmed hat, black patent stilettos, gypsy scarf and chain smoking) on Mill Street in Bideford. These and many other things had been swirling around in my mind for some months. Added to this I had been charged with organising a ceremony to deposit the South Western Arrow in a place of power. For months I felt uncomfortable, as though snared by a briar, whichever way I twisted to find the key, the answer, I found myself more tightly caught in this network of symbols. Roses, pilgrimages, 156, black Africa, a dream of a secret place in which the arrow must be put.

Frater Cephalopoda and I did a working and attempted to invoke wisdom from the dream world. I was given the name of our western temple – the name of the Rose[2]. I also dreamt that the arrow needed to be put 'somewhere that wasn't obviously important' – I'd run through places this could be, my unconscious symbolised this as a hole in a girder (a location that was reached by going up a magick tree and through a series of curiously deserted shopping malls). Did this mean we should leave this talisman on the Oldenburg, that sails from Bideford quay to the Isle of Lundy? Or perhaps somewhere hidden in the Town's new quayside building; an architectural abortion of New Labour maritime influenced design? And how, if at all, did Pomba Gira fit into this?

---

1   See *Chaos International* No 25 & Chapter 1 of
     Now That's What I Call Chaos Magick.
2   Temple Rosa Mundi

When I first moved to Bideford I'd performed the usual web searches, consulting the volumes of the internet, that most mobile and shifting of unseen libraries. There I discovered the work of the historian Frank Gent and his publication of original trial transcripts and commentary on the Bideford witches – the last people in England to be hanged for the crime of *malefica*. I'd read the book as soon as I arrived in town and was disappointed. These weren't real witches. No genuine lingering Old Religion here, no shadows of women's magick or even mysterious paranormal goings on. No; the story of the Bideford witches seemed to be an everyday tale of prejudice, violence, hypocrisy and scapegoating. Like a witch finder myself I'd been after the genuine article and instead found the classic ethnographer's social phenomenon – a witch-hunt pure and simple.

But as the time for the ritual came closer I re-read the text. Yes, there was something of value here – the scapegoat. Again I wandered the internet and the books in my own collection, learning about the Jewish ritual of the scapegoat, of the animal bearing the sins of the community set free to wander into 'Azazel' (a term of uncertain etymology but with the ring of demonology about it). I realised that this is what Pomba Gira is the goddess of, the underdog, the oppressed, those on skid row. She is the scapegoat of culture, the sacrificed, whether she is the elderly woman, the woman crippled with childbearing, or the maid 'too pretty for her own good'.

Through her power we would find the location for the arrow. Through her incandescent sexuality we would send our power back into time. Perhaps we could unpick the scapegoating of the witch craze, maybe we could drive the arrow even deeper to challenge or change the very basis of this response. Perhaps this ritual would be a catharsis the Order needed, time to bury old enmities, to heal wounds to the Pact? Maybe we might be able to find ways of ritualising our need to scapegoat so that we could minimise the harm done? Whatever the outcomes, we needed to meet this process head-on.

On the afternoon of the 17th of April 2004 personnel began to assemble at my home. From East, West, South and North – Frater Cephalopoda and I had prepared the spaces in which we would work. I tried as best I could to keep my energy level under control. Sleeplessness, excitement, long-distance driving and parenting had left me somewhat manic. By the time my guests began to arrive I had a sense that we were ready, the stage was set, now it remained to see who the players might be.

Frater Axis, Frater Quanta, Soror Macha, Frater Elijah, Frater PicaPica, Frater Encephla, Frater Fantastic, Frater Mind Fire and Frater Ahperl arrived, each person coming with their own story, their own style and their own inimitable brand of magick.

Food and socialising over we began to get to work. Outside, the rain fell and the sky was darkening. All eleven of us were forced into close proximity by the small rooms of my 18th century house, the walls listening to the tale I wanted to tell.

Frater Cephalopoda and I explained the basis of our ceremony. All players had already been briefed to bring offerings suitable for Pomba Gira; vials of perfume, blunts, talismans of her veves, fruit, and tequila were to be her gifts. Though I had expected more Sisters to be present the fact that we were ten men and one woman was significant. I'd already approached Soror Macha and asked if she would be prepared to be the horse of the Orisha. She agreed and had prepared herself by coming equipped with a range of regalia suitable for the Goddess of Whores.

Pomba Gira manifests in a variety of forms, some shading off into Venusian eroticism, some into protective Martian guises. Tonight we would work with a slightly more Saturnine face of the Goddess – Pomba Gira of the Seven Crossroads mixes elements of Lillith with Erzulie, her sacred place is the graveyard and she is the guardian of thresholds and liminalspaces - feminina del eshu.

Frater Fantastic had also prepared a working – a pathworking which would fit perfectly with my proposal (and physically would not challenge our limitations of space). This would be an astral discovery and creation of the Temple Omega space, a location with a physical form (a curiously neglected zone in Leeds) and a place of power for all present to participate in.

As night fell we trooped off to 'the shed', a temple space in my garden. The rain was falling and a cold wind travelled down the valley. Once inside a chaos vortex was opened. The fire in the wood burner and our

93

bodies gave the room pleasant warmth. Frater Fantastic led us through the pathworking – traversing space from the orbital space station of Octarine Power Force 5 through to the subterranean realms of chaotic power deep within the earth.

After this Frater Cephalopoda led us through a session of over breathing and shaking. Each of us tingling with power, we then sat in silence while Fr Cephalopoda delivered prayers from the Church of Santa Daime. In the language that Pomba Gira would be most familiar with, Portuguese, we asked for the blessing of the Divine on our work.

Other prayers were offered and then one by one the participants were led out of the room.

I led Frater Cephalopoda out first so that he could make ready our second space, lighting candles and incense in the subterranean temple. Next Soror Macha was invited out, to give her time to change into her costume.

As I guided each person from the room, eyes closed, down the path back towards the house they were met by Frater Cephalopoda, asked to disrobe and then led into the very earth of North Devon. As I ferried each participant I would glance up. From the bedroom window came a red light; the whore was preparing herself.

Ten naked men sat on the earth. The goddess descended. High heels rapping on each step, cane in hand, long black hair spilling down her back.

Frater Cephalopoda began to clap and chant "Pomba Gira". I lit a cigarillo and began my invocation:

Opener of the way

Threshold woman

Lady of the night

Mother of demons

Wanton mother of the world

Pomba Gira, feminina del eshu, maria de las siete encrsliadas,

Pomba Gira, feminina del eshu, maria de las siete encrsliadas,

Pomba Gira, feminina del eshu, maria de las siete encrsliadas,

Ashe, ashe, ashe

We make offerings to you – we ask that you come to our aid, mother of the darkness, patroness of the downtrodden, sexy goddess of delightful sin, delightful slut of ecstasy!

Within moments of entering the room I could tell that the Horse was feeling the effects of the rite. It was as though the time and place had been waiting for this, as though she was just below the surface and only a little work was required to open the floodgates – Pomba Gira began to pace the circle, brandishing her cane, snarling and cursing.

"So you want something from me boys eh?

YOU WANT SOMETHING FROM ME?

Well what are you prepared to give me?"

A flurry of activity as we offer her items on the altar. Tobacco, cannabis, finally tequila seems to hit the mark.

"Ah get the hooker drunk is it?"

I offered Pomba Gira a glass of spirit, raving and pacing she spun around, spraying us all with the alcohol from her snarling lips.

"Help us Pomba Gira, show us the way across the crossroads, help us"

A cacophony of drums, chanting, cries and hands thrust upward offering gifts. Pomba Gira dances, wheels around in the centre of the circle.

"When patriarchy came, replacing the former matriarchal system, the co-operative model was abandoned."

"I wasn't going to lie beneath Adam, that stinking shrivelled worm!"

"Yes I am angry but that anger has had many years to cool down."

"WHAT DO YOU SAY?"

We begin to say it; "Sorry, Pomba Gira"

"WHAT FOR?"

For what happened. For the scapegoating, for the sacrifice of women, for the crushing of those who gave birth to us, for turning away from the feminine, the collective, for our own cruelty and ignorance and stupidity.

Show us the way! I take up the arrow and offer it to the Goddess, all hands are upon her body as she gyrates. I press the arrow to her yoni and she presses against it, taking it up to her mouth, holding it and suffusing it with her power. For this weapon is part of the chaotic diaspora, a scattering of components across the landscape and this goddess is Queen of the dispossessed.

What was her teaching? Dislocated fragments:

"Follow the fire in your belly – follow the fire serpent

Use your group intelligence, a network of minds that can process far more than one consciousness"

Again hands upon the body of Pomba Gira, male hands holding her up as she circles in trance and with a cry she drops to the floor. We prepare to make our pilgrimage out into Bideford town, back into the past of the place that sacrificed three women to the hatred of the mob.

Outside it is raining. We dress. Soror Macha lets the invocation smoulder within her – a 'fire in her belly'. Under the bridge we meet a hedgehog, totem beast of Scorpio. At the cross roads on the eastern side of the bridge we make an offering of a red rose and I recall the names of the three women that died; Suzanne Edwards, Mary Trembles and Temperance Lloyd. Soror Macha lets a red rose fall, it hits the mud beside the skeleton form of a shopping trolley. Collars turned up against the rain; across the nine hundred year old bridge we hit the town on Saturday night.

At the western end of the bridge, by the spot where the lock-up stood in which Temperance Lloyd was 'overheard' confessing to the curses she had laid, another offering is made. From this quay (at which, on that night a large cargo vessel was moored) men had set sail to a New World with avarice in their hearts. A rose falls into the turbulent river below us.

Then into town, down narrow alleys, snippets of pub conversation, bright lights, laughter, the smells of chips and beer. Young women, impervious to the cold and damp, totter down the road giggling.

Another rose is left poking out of a cash point on the spot where Temperance Lloyd allegedly met the 'Black Man' – the Devil.

Along Mill Street, a narrow arcade of shop and pubs, to Lower Gunstone Street on the corner of which stands the Heavitree Arms. Heavitree, the little hamlet outside Exeter, on the south coast of Devon where the witches were executed.

Then a steep climb to the top of the western hill, through Old Town. To a crossroads just beyond which stood the cottages where people said the witches used to live. This was burnt to the ground in the mid nineteenth century, an arson perhaps motivated by a supposed diabolic crime perpetrated over one hundred and fifty years previously.

Then past The Lamb Inn (shades of Henry Durbin's investigation of 'witchcraft' in eighteenth century Bristol) and down towards the Pannier Market, the economic heart of this once rich town. Here Soror Macha lays the rose alone, pushing it between the bars of the gate to Butchers Row, her silhouette a frightening figure of loss and desire, walking alone across the road in the night. More and more I get that characteristic feeling, as though each seen I witness is a panel in a graphic novel. We have left the Apparent World and are cruising through Archetypal Reality.

Then down the steps of an ancient road towards 'Holy Mother Church'. The tower rises before us as we turn the corner, crowned with the flag of St.George, a huge illuminated cross and a great golden cockerel, Voudoun symbols of the crossroads writ large above us.

We enter the graveyard. Here is the place that should have taught compassion and kindness and instead managed to preside over the terrible crimes of the witchhunt.

Through the northern gate we make our entrance, past the grave of a woman who died in her eighth childbirth.

What do we do here?

"Confess our sins" says Frater Fantastic.

Pomba Gira asks us to confess our crimes, as men, as part of history and in doing so we become our own scapegoats, our own saviours and make the right choices at the crossroads. The rain falls, the light from the illuminated cross and deep shadows from the yew trees give the graveyard an odd aspect. Like a figure from a gothic romance Soror Macha steps forward and lays the final rose upon a tomb.

Hands are placed upon the arrow, like a ouja plachette it begins to move, seeking out the right place. We are pulled by the fetish as it wriggles and points widdershins around the church from north to south. We are pressed closer and closer together, as one body we squeeze around the path that circumambulates the church.

Then the spot is near, the arrow veers off the path into a grove of trees. Knotted together, hands reaching to stay connected, rain falling and dark in the shadows, we find the spot. Together we squat beneath the trees, mixed odours of earth and dog shit, our hands raise and the arrow is buried in the ground. Soror Macha screams.

We emerge again and salute the Grove of the Arrow. The energy is draining away from us, Frater Axis gives a formal licence to depart. "Take the wig off" he says.

Pomba Gira had done her work.

Back to the temple (no rest for the wicked), for a rite of Insubordination (of Frater Ahperl by Frater Fantastic), and finally my wonderfully brave novices get to be formally introduced to the assembled company. Later that night other magick is done – a spontaneous sigil casting to bring great success to the IOT Seminars. In my addled state I can neither sleep nor wake. A strange edgy energy still seems to be flowing through me, shivers like mushroom energy rushes, bouts of paranoia, the dark edges and hissing of potential fainting. Does something else need doing? I've been close to this type of explosive energy before – last time was in Brighton. One destroyed working group and one temple conflagration later, I was unnerved to think a repeat performance might be had in my home.

Frater Ahperl, inspired by a quantity of intoxicants, burnt the sigil and it was flung into the washing up bowl. This was the time to earth the whole shebang. I took the remains of the sigil, floating in the greasy water, out into the garden and threw it into the air. A glass bowl that had been hidden beneath the water went flying too and smashed on the path.

After that, my energy began to smooth out a little. Perhaps this simple act of destruction (plus the traditional Macumba technique of removing a vessel of water, and with it any un-discharged energy from a place, was all that was needed. Through that act, and the acupressure ministrations of Soror Macha I was able to let this one go.

The morning brought with it Chi Gong and a return to the temple. Discussions and an octarine burst directed towards 'all those falsely imprisoned' by Frater Axis. The energy that had swept us all up so quickly the night before was discharged, leaving a blessing of protection on those travelling home that day.

Outside the rain had stopped. The storm was over.

movement and sound, help hold the focus and direction of the rite together, and can help us navigate the challenging territory of the visionary state successfully. In my experience using cannabis is ideal when it comes to psychogeographical (and indeed much magickal work). Once the effects of cannabis become familiar, or to put it another way, when the spirit becomes one of the magickians allies, it is a superb material to journey with. Walking ceremonies might also be started or finished with the use of major psychedelics or indeed for short-lived materials (such as smoked DMT) punctuated by psychedelic events.

With another magician I've been walking the landscape – tapping into those icons of magical travel, Ve, the wandering form of Odin, the tarot trump The Hermit, the myth of the journey, the quest. Along the coat of Hartland in Devon, across the Bodmin moor, we have been mythologising these and other landscapes. What we meet in our journeys; people, obstacles, delights, we are engaging with real things that mirror our interior, occult, unconscious minds.

On many of these walks we have used, in the broadest sense, the chaos approach to magick. We have arrived with a few materials; chalks, old pieces of jewellery, ribbons, candles, and rattles. For different sections of the walk we would select a technique; mantra, crawling low over the ground (sniffing and literally tasting the place) or other methods to change our consciousness – to tune into the spirit of the place. At our stopping points we made art, shrines, curious fetishes, features that celebrated the place and declared its sanctity to those who would come after us.

For me this process also exemplified one of the core elements of chaos magick practice. When we talk about chaos magick we are not so much talking about the particular use of a set of symbols (though of course the history of chaos magick is an accretion of elements that can be mistaken for its core) as much as a certain approach, a set of tactics. The ability to move fluidly from one belief system to another, from one way of modifying awareness (creating trance) to another is essential in chaos magick. At a temple ritual a number of participants might bring different practises or rituals to do. So in psychogeographical work we respond directly to the landscape and bring our repertoire of techniques to the field: We might use a breathing method, a visualisation (being pulled along by our HGA), crawling and experiencing the world through smell and taste, mantra and whatever other methods we have at our disposal. The aim of all these techniques is to create unity of awareness in the mind and to unify our desire (to contact and commune with the spirit of the land) with our being – to resolve this lack into manifestation. So a wide variety of techniques can be deployed in the psychogeographical adventure.

Chaos magick practitioners have been noted for their emphasis on results and this is especially evident in the now widely employed approach of sigilisation. The creating of glyphs that are then charged with power and then 'launched' has its own parallels in psychogeographic work. But in this system, when we need something we go and get it. For instance, a working to enhance communication might involve a ritual pilgrimage to a telecommunications tower. A ceremony to gain the aid and powers of a specific animal spirit might require us to seek out the actual home of that animal and spend some time there. I did some work about a year ago to work with the spirit of the magpie. The initial ceremony was conducted using a shamanic psychogeographical approach. I spent some time reading up and getting familiar with the legends and lore of the magpie and then when the time was right went for a walk. I took with me a lamen or talisman I had created which was to form the visual connection to the spirit ally. I approached the mission like a character from Carlos Castaneda, stalking power through the landscape. Eventually I ended up crawling on my hands and knees under some blackthorn bushes all the way into a dense thicket of spikes. Here I found a small space in which I was able to offer my prayer and power to the spirit to ask it to become my ally. As soon as I had finished the rite there was a laugh behind me as though another human was present. I turned around and through a tunnel formed by the trees I could see movement.

I crawled through the tunnel and eventually emerged into a sunlit glade, protected on all sides by the thorny barrier. There dancing and hopping on the grass were two magpies – two for joy! They gave me a spirit song to help me with my work and an intuition about how to call on them, and how to feed them power. The technique that the journey provided me with was one of empty handed magick – ie requiring no physical props, and having already used the journey to make contact with the spirit in its own world, also required little or no major alterations in consciousness to be effectively cast.

In another act of weaving I've been walking with my family. Sometimes our baby on my back, sometimes in his fabulous chariot. On these journeys we have walked the points of the compass at the solstices and equinoxes. Each journey would provide us with a magical talisman, something that would be found at the farthest point of the walk and would then be taken back to our home. On a subsequent walk that talisman would be taken, moving like the shuttle on the loom, out in another direction. Then we would place that power object at the end of the walk and find the next token. Each found object – a rusty nail, an old box of mathematical instruments, a crab apple sit on one of our household altars until the year turns and it's time to return it to the magical landscape in which we live.

The acts of weaving, of shrine making, of deliberate pilgrimages make us aware of the sacredness of the planet and the place we inhabit. We begin to understand ourselves as both archetypal presence in the landscape – the Stranger, the shaman, the pilgrim, and as temporary, transient beings. In those places where one passes through the urban landscape it is possible to glimpse the sacred in the gutter, the demonic and divine in the brickwork. In those places where there are fewer buildings there is a sense that we are walking the new song lines of our culture.

Obviously our psychogeography cannot be uncritical, and although we might mythologise our landscape we should be very prepared to enter into it through other approaches and these methods can support our endeavours. Learning the history, the biology, the geology and archaeology of a place gives us more material to make the world sacred and need not be opposed to our artistry. The idea that the world rides on vast giants called tectonic plates is a supremely evocative image. The awareness that river meander or that ancient ice flows gouged shapes in the land are awesome, sublime perceptions. As we mythologise the landscape we should do so with humour (an element that is common within the chaos magick approach) and a degree of humility (perhaps less common!). For whatever we make of the world is fleeting and our little human consciousness can be swept away by the merest shudder in the planet upon which we stand.

By doing these journeys we are literally re-making the world, re-creating and re-enchanting space here and now. That which is common place, humdrum, becomes invigorated and enriched with a poetic perception. We are stalking power, finding our place, seeking an environment of pleasure, freedom and power.

The Magickal Art of Drugs

(A paper delivered at the Exploring Consciousness conference June 2004 at The Sophia Centre at Bath Spa University College and Psychonaut UK.)

I'd like to begin this presentation by explaining my understanding of what magick is. I'm going to provide an overview of the development of the Western Occult Tradition and then show how and why the emerging technology of magick can be deployed with particular regard to pharmacological approaches to self discovery.

So what is magick?

For me, as I have explained in my book *Pharmakon,* occultism *is the study and practice of engaging with mystery.* Magick is the technology of exploring the occult, those hidden aspects of the universe. Magick provides mechanisms whereby we can learn to cause changes in the observable processes of the universe by interacting with the 'invisible' realm of mystery. Today we might describe some of these changes as 'psychological', others we might call parapsychological.

Occultism is quintessentially the study of the world of the between: between fact and phantasy, between divine and demonic, between matter and mind. Occult experimenters, those people who deploy its methods as 'magick', position themselves in this liminal space. If we are seeking to understand consciousness (especially in cultures where there is an apparent split between matter and mind), magick can be a powerful ally, for it is this space between duality that is its natural habitat.

The occult tradition exists as the esoteric body of knowledge within many different beliefs. Within classical Paganism it existed as Thergia, within Christianity as Gnosticism, within Islam as Sufism. The key point is that these esoteric, mystical, magickal discourses within a larger religion are crucially about praxis. They are based less on doctrinal knowledge but instead emphasise the experiential. These are bodies of technique, of experiment and exploration clothed in the language of the religion into which they are woven.

Today, occultism is beginning to emerge on its own terms. For occultism is a study, an area of enquiry that, whilst it may utilise the language of religion or science (or art, or many other things), is itself a complete body of knowledge.

The grandfather of contemporary Western occultism is undoubtedly Eliphas Levi, who attempted to formulate a general theory of magick (indeed he always claimed to be primarily a theorist rather than a practitioner of the occult arts). It was Levi's *The Dogma and Ritual of High Magic* (1856) that began the process of de-coupling magick from any specifically religious viewpoint. Levi sought to cut through the complexity of the subject in order to identify 'principles'. What he was doing for occultism, his contemporaries were also doing in creating a scientific language (devoid of explicitly religious content) to explain such phenomena as mesmerism.

Levi's first principle of magick was that of the Will which, as in mesmerism, was imagined 'as steam or the galvanic current', that is as a 'real' force. Levi suggested that paraphernalia such as robes, incense, magick circles and the like were primarily important as aids in supporting the Will. Their virtue was in their effect on the Will of the magician and not primarily from any inherent property. With this principle Levi, at a stroke, jettisoned the magician's reliance on virgin parchment and the blood of pigeons, and recast the material mechanics of magick into what the 20th century occultist Israel Regardie would later call 'an artificial system of props and aids'.

Levi's second principle was that of the astral light. This light was the medium or dimension of reality which permeated all things, and of which the material world was only one of innumerable projections. Levi's conception of the astral light was similar to ideas such as that of the luminiferous ether (the medium through which electromagnetic radiation was conjectured to pass by 19th century physicists) and the all-pervasive 'odic force' of Baron von Reichenbach. The fundamental principle of magick that the doctrine of the astral light reaffirmed was 'all is one and one is all'– everything in the universe was intimately interconnected. Today we might well describe this astral light using the mythology of quantum mechanics.

Levi's third principle concerned correspondences or 'like attracts like', what James Frazer went on to examine in *The Golden Bough* as 'sympathetic magic'.

For Levi the doctrine of 'as above, so below' affirmed that what was within the macrocosm was reflected within the microcosm. Today models such as the holographic or fractal universe expound essentially the same belief. On the most superficial level one might say that humans are 'the magickal mirror of the universe' so that the constellation of Leo related to the breast and the organ of the heart. However, for Levi these chains of symbolic meaning were not to be taken strictly literally, rather it was the principle or quality that these symbols represented that would have a sympathy or connection. Thus, the principle represented by the god Mars would correspond with activities such as conflict and qualities such as passion in the soul of the magician. It was this conception of the doctrine of correspondences that paved the way for the dream analysis of psychoanalysis and the archetypes of Carl Jung.

Following Levi, groups such as The Hermetic Order of The Golden Dawn successfully nurtured the growth of occultism as a corpus of knowledge. The schema of the Qabalah formed the primary skeleton upon which this body was fleshed out. The doctrine of correspondences expanded utilising concepts, myths and images drawn from ancient Egyptian religion, Classical symbolism, Buddhist meditations and a formidable range of other sources to create an extensive and coherent system. What was happening here was the recreation (in a modern context) of a language of the imagination, a series of metaphorical associations, not 'true' in themselves but pointing to the process that has been called the re-enchantment of the world. No longer was the universe composed of discrete, separate objects, rather it could be seen as a fabric of meaning and association, woven together by the power of the imagination.

The adepts of the Golden Dawn emphasised the principle of imagination in magickal work. They suggested that the Will was blind and impotent unless the Imagination had been sufficiently developed by practices such as visualisation. The Will and Imagination were seen as the twin forces that accomplished magick. By furnishing the Imagination with the correct symbolic vocabulary, through knowledge of correspondences, mental images thus created could be given reality by the controlled use of the Will.

It was during the 1970s, with the second phase of the modern occult revival in full swing, that the depth and range of esoteric systems appearing in the West made it increasingly hard to justify using only one approach (such as the Qabalah based iconography of post-Golden Dawn magick). The increasing amount of information emerging about Eastern occultism, as well as new scientific developments (for instance in parapsychology and quantum physics) led researchers to propose another two key magickal principles. The contribution of these additional principles was closely linked to the emergence of the school known as chaos magick. There were:

Belief shifting - The method of the operation (ie magickal work) is not as important as one's firm belief in its effectiveness. Belief shifting was a principle that was particularly in tune with the emergence of post-modernist philosophy into mainstream culture (in the 1980s). Belief (and the ability to adopt different beliefs) seemed to be the factor that combined Will and Imagination and framed the space within which magick could take place.

Gnosis - The operation should be conducted in an altered state of consciousness. Whether through biofeedback, dance, sex, psychedelics or any number of other methods, entering a 'trance' state appeared to be a key element in successful magick. Today, generating and successfully managing various states of gnosis is seen as pivotal to the pursuit of any magickal practice.

So how can the emerging body of knowledge that magick comprises enhance the use of drugs to explore consciousness?

Ladies and gentlemen, these are truly blessed days – our species has created and catalogued a vast array of chemicals that can radically change the way our minds operate. From the ancient ayahuasca beverage to laboratory synthesised materials such as MDMA, if we are interested in using pharmacological methods of exploring consciousness then we have the greatest array of allies in our journey.

Within many different communities we see drugs being considered as a legitimate method of enquiry and exploration, aids in discovering who we are – from the academic and scientific community through to groups such as the Red Path and the Santo Diame church, and in wider society, through rave culture. Even in those countries where the government is vehemently anti-drugs many of these materials are ubiquitous – personally I'm sure that I could step outside this room and within a few hours score a variety of powerful, illegal consciousness changing agents.

Why are drugs so interesting when it comes to exploring consciousness? Well one answer is because, like magick, they occupy a liminal space. A drug is an objective material, yet its effect is primarily subjective. Moreover the nature of the subjective effect is a blend of three intertwined variables – set, setting and substance. Like consciousness itself, a drug's effect exists partly within the molecule and the nerve synapse, partly in the expectations and predispositions of the individual mind of the user and partly in those relationships between the individual and their environment. It is the subjectivity and, indeed, the variability of drug experience that makes it so interesting.

At this conference we have an assembly of many investigators who take the subjective seriously, who would undoubtedly have laughed in the face of B.F. Skinner's assertion that there is no such thing as consciousness. We have people such as Susan Blackmore who, in her quest to understand the phenomena of alien abduction has personally subjected herself to extreme magnetic effects to experience the subjective changes that result. We have Alexander Shulgin, the alchemist who, with his circle of adventurers, has explored numerous new psychedelic materials and Benny Shannon who has developed a rich and deep relationship with the ayahuasca brew and closely analysed that experience through the tradition of phenomenology.

In all these cases it is the re-valuing of the subjective realm that is critical to these people's work.

And it is in this emphasis on the subjective that we all share, that I believe magick has a role to play.

Magickal techniques can help us interact with and discover the contents of the occult, subjective, 'imaginal realm'. This realm is the place of the metaphorical rather than the literal. Rather than trying to circumvent the subjective realm, as attempts at objective experimental science have done, magick embraces this space and seeks to deploy a wide variety of approaches to explore this world.

So when a belief says 'there is a sleeping serpent, coiled three and a half times around the base of your spine' only a fool would take this literally and call the zoo, or dismiss this statement as coming from the biologically ignorant. The magickian says "Hey that's great, what happens when she wakes up, and how should I feed her to keep her happy?" So for Kundalini yoga we have the paradigm, the envelope or context within which a subjective effect happens, and the magickal techniques themselves (visualisation, mantra, paranayama) are the methods for navigating this world. Engaging with the metaphorical language of the belief, and deploying these techniques to explore it, is the magickal approach.

And one key point about magick, about this practice of manipulating and learning from the imaginal realm, is that anyone can do it. Essential human processes such as the development of a successful theory of mind, rely on the imaginative process, they rely on us all finding ways to navigate the imaginative, subjective world. In just the same way that a sane waking life depends on being able to dream, so attempts to create an objective world, to inhabit our cultural, inter-subjective reality, necessitate the existence of the imaginal world. I believe that imagination is the link between our inner and outer world, and in some senses we might say that consciousness itself is primarily structured through the imaginative ability. It is the creation of a consistent, apparently external world built from our inner memories and the external input of our senses.

Consciousness is enfolded in the world, it is part of the world, so techniques of creating apparently objective knowledge about it (ie Popparian science), however valuable, can only illuminate certain aspects of what it is. Clearly some approaches to any given phenomena are better suited to exploring some aspects of it than others. (What use would it be if an art critic only talked about the chemical composition of the paint used by an artist?)

This emphasis on the subjective realm and techniques of accessing and exploring it (what I have called magickal techniques) is essential if we are not to miss out on some splendid opportunities for discovery. Especially when we come to deploy those great changers of consciousness – drugs.

As an example; in the UK at the moment there are a series of experiments being conducted using ketamine. The aim of the experiments is to look at the dissassociative effects of ketamine and to examine these using Functional magnetic resonance imaging (fMRI) techniques. The subjects that have been chosen for these experiments have been carefully screened so that they have as little drug experience as possible. When the ketamine is administered it will be in the usual double blind way but the doses used will be very low.

Now this experiment may well yield useful and interesting results, and I don't doubt for a moment the capability of the team undertaking it. But let's think about this – why use ketamine in this experiment? Well because of how it makes you *feel* - in this case, disassociated. If this is the case, why only choose people who have no previous experience of this feeling, or indeed of any (illegal) drug induced dissociation? The raison d'être of using this drug is because users *feel* dissociated – but to fail to engage directly with this subjective experience is a sad lack in this enquiry. It is as though we have decided that we are interested in understanding how art works on the human brain, so we have gathered together a group of people who have hardly been exposed to art before and have never set foot inside a gallery. We have asked them to wear sunglasses so they don't get too high a dose of the art and then rather than asking them what they made of their, admittedly, impoverished tour of the gallery we limited ourselves to looking at the results of an EEG trace from each subject.

So how, in practice, would an understanding of the importance of the subjective, imaginal realm and the magickal techniques used to address it, change an experiment such as this?

In the case of the ketamine experiment this would mean including experienced psychonauts in the study, giving equal value to the subjective accounts that subjects produced, as well as the fMRI data, also developing useful ways of interpreting and analysing these texts, and indeed exploring the deployment of non-drug methods of changing consciousness (for example asking ketamine explorers to try paranayama methods during their voyage) and examining how these modify the ketamine experience. Crucially the experiment, if it is particularly interested in the phenomena of disassociation, would explore more deeply the individual subject's notions and experience of this phenomena before the experiment. Our minds are not tabula rasa and even though someone may never have had a drug induced disassociative experience that does not mean that they will not have experiences and expectations that will significantly modify how they relate to the ketamine when it hits.

I think that increasingly we shall see a move away from the idea that Drug X=Experience Y and instead an emphasis on exploring the set and setting rather than substance components of any given drug experience. In the world of subjective exploration it ain't what you do, it's the way that you do it. Techniques derived from shamanismsm and tribal cultures will cross fertilise with insights generated by contemporary scientific practice.

I believe the next step for our community is not the creation of yet more novel materials or the discovery of previously unknown organic psychedelics (although there is of course value in this avenue of enquiry). It's not a question of new drugs, rather a question of deploying these in different contexts, using those technologies of the imaginal realm to explore the interaction of the mind and molecules. Drugs provide us with one of the great laboratories to explore our selves, and when combined with the techniques of magick they can be the fuel that allows us to venture into the hidden architecture of consciousness. The process of successfully blending these elements together is why I describe this as an art.

The use of the term art recalls Aleister Crowley's definition of magic as being both an "..art and science". Artists, as Oliver Sacks points out, are "the antennae of culture"

I believe that drugs, wisely used, can provide humanity with a new art. I believe that drugs are an important way to renew and revive our global culture. A culture that legitimised the use of drugs would be a culture that did not fear change. A society that validated and encouraged transformative experience would be a 'spiritual' culture. It wouldn't be a static utopia with everything 'sorted', rather it would be an environment where individuals could move towards authenticity and self-actualisation - a society that was both challenged by, but also supportive of, these goals.

And this is a culture that we are all helping to forge, right here, right now.

Magick with a K

We are inside a tepee, Soror Macha and I. We've just returned from the Exploring Consciousness Conference after-party. Already present in our bodies is around 100mg of MDMA each, plus half a 2-CI pill (a new one on both of us). The effects are still present though our drop time was some hours ago. Now we're here, snug inside this elegant conical space.

"So what do you want to do?"

"Well…we could do some K."

A tiny, beautifully made image of Ganesh sits atop the micro stereo. The music is cued and ready to go. The floor of the tepee is covered in colourful rugs, sheepskins and blankets; a temporal autonomous comfort zone.

A few nightlights stand on the floor (not necessarily the wisest form of illumination given the nature of our proposed experiment). From one pole of the tepee a lantern casts a lattice of shadow and shapes of pinkish light around the facets of canvas.

Soror Macha prepares the sacrament; white crystals glinting on a mirror, a rolled banknote.

It is time to pray. First a Sanskrit prayer to Ganesha, then in English:

Great Fat God of beginnings, fill us with your happiness.

Open the way for us,

Protect our ceremony

Break down all obstacles in our path!

OM GAM.

"We take this ketamine", says Soror Macha, "with the intention of understanding more fully the K experience. You first."

I take the mirror and snort the white powder. Without the anesthetising effect of cocaine I can feel a huge wad of material jam up my left nostril.

My partner takes her line.

Now there is no safe word – what will be will be. The music begins, sound just audible. Outside dawn is breaking, we move onto the bed, fully clothed.

"How do you want to sit?"

"Yab Yum."

We get comfortable and embrace. I feel the human, solid form of my Sister, my hands noticing ribs, expanses of muscles, the texture of cotton. Our faces come together and we begin to exchange breath – in and out, merging our energies, creating a cycle of prana between our bodies. Our hands move over each other and there is comfort in that embrace. Yet I begin to sense a hesitation, a sense of awkwardness. I feel less confident, less relaxed but I know that this is a sign, that deep in my body systems are beginning to register a change. This provokes a sting of adrenaline, and its characteristic tightening up, before the full force of the K overpowers it. Something is changing, something is on the move, my neurochemistry gears itself up for yet another intervention – it begins.

We are moving. Sliding our hands and bodies around, then we begin to sway gently. All hesitation, all unease has evaporated, we are anemones swaying in the current of a warm ocean. Our bodies echo the neurological undoing that is taking place. The ketamine relaxes us, eyes close. As my shoulder presses against that of Soror Macha my mind is intensely drawn into that sensation – pressure, warmth, texture. I am falling into a black hole, pulled toward the singularity of that sensation, that atom to atom contact between my body and that of my companion. I am acutely conscious of the location of this feeling, this isn't an all-in-the-brain 'neural representation', instead the feeling is profoundly embodied and embedded in my body. Yet my body is simultaneously disappearing, or rather it is becoming harder to define the limits of it. All is one, one is all in a literal, corporeal sense. Surfaces of touch give way – our bodies are blended and the physical sensations are both seen and sensed clearly in visual terms. First black and white designs, then blue enters the imagery, then light of many different colours. Multihued surfaces that bend and buckle as they move, cells burst and flood into one another, membranes rupture, tectonic plates are subducted and plunge downwards towards more of the same. Turtle shells composed of morphing, conical Platonic solids – all the way down…

Soror Macha lies backwards and I bend forward. My mind briefly attempts to establish my 'true' position – am I squashing her? Is there sufficient blood flow to my legs? With eyes open I can see the room, but unlike the same experience on, say, LSD, the apparent world isn't pregnant with meaning or rendered radically alien. I can see the pillows, our bags, yet they are seen as though through a haze. This haze isn't literal (there is no visual confusion of overlaid grids as might be seen on mushrooms) but figurative. Objects have no interest for me, they evoke no response, they are only things.

I close my eyes and am pulled down the K-hole, brightly coloured surfaces of meaning roll down like industrial conveyor belts. Down at the bottom of one layer I am I within the deep places of the earth. Rich visions in LED glowing green, shapes like markings on circuit boards, ghostly glowing like the controls of a strange, organic machine.

There are presences here too. Consciousness, the background hum of persons unseen, like me - disembodied. Is this the realm of the ancestors, these billion calm ghost voices? For a moment I am interrupted, here are fuzzy, angular, splintering, crunching shapes. These are forms of residual fear. I pass through them and there is a sense of the divine (much like that I have experienced with Santo Diame). I am aware that my head is resting on Soror Macha's chest, and in my vision my head is bowed in prayer. I am adoring a blue black goddess, her body is composed of infinite space and the infinite stars. My own body is now completely and easily jettisoned. Time is ever coming, infinite, and palpably present; all being is eternal doing.

And it is okay to die.

Now the first stage of the return.

We become lucid for a moment and re-arrange our bodies, lying together under the blankets. I am now aware of the earthly nature of this spirit, of verdant fractating ferns. Outside and across the music (of which I am hardly aware) birds sing in real-time.

As the feeling begins to fade I become aware of how much the tepee poles perfectly capture the relationship of surfaces in many parts of the vision. One structure, divided into many faces, each intersecting, interacting and stretched towards one infinite point (the increasingly blue sky above us). In K there are lines rather than the mandala circles that dominate the imagery of drugs such as LSD. K is so abstract, so refined that it presents the equivalent of 'clean lines, modern living' to the house party hippy style of acid. K is also (in this voyage at least) little inclined to produce anything as direct and intelligible as a realistic vision. The figures and events, the dream-like content that most psychoactives can produce is absent from ketamine. No resplendent psychedelic temples, no erotic writhing forms (that mushrooms are apt to create), no multi-roomed castles in the air (as with ayahuasca). But here there is a sense of purpose in the experience itself, though this sense is not alluded to by archetypal imagery. This is a manifestation of familiar power, regal and strong. Ketamine means something. She doesn't indulge in the fizzy pop of memory, grabbing old content and re-arranging it to make her point. Not does she demonstrate the astonishing breadth and depth of human creativity as ayahuasca is able to do. K explains herself through images but these images are the visual analogue of kinaesthetic feeling. She gets to you directly through the body. The armour of habitual posture (both literal and metaphorical) is breached. Knots of tension slide away, and beneath these tics and habits, in each joint, in the junction between each cell – there is the pure process of movement. Some claim that fundamentally our consciousness is predicated on our ability to move, to be active agents in the world, movement determines awareness. As we move our bodies the fact of our locomotion is translated instantly through all cells in the body (if nothing else by changes in gravitational pull, velocity and so forth). So our sense of movement is a global sense, a full body knowledge that K can get into and release, open and re-configure.

K is gentle but distant. She doesn't come rushing up like the mushroom spirit. Her aloof attitude reminds me somewhat of LSD (though acid is far less a clear personality for me) or perhaps the 'Green Goddess' of Salvia Divinorum (another drug noted for its curious effect on body awareness). Though distant there is still a sense of caring in ketamine, a reserved but definite love. She isn't Venus, but more like Binah, that great Mother of Time, Nuit the cosmic or stellar divinity.

My eyes open and I watch the day creep brighter into the sky, a few droplets of rain are falling through the central hole of the tepee.

Like a good friend leaving – she is going, the ketamine experience retreats; so sad to see her go.

Aware of the vast volume of snot from my nose I begin to sense my body but there isn't any rush. I have a sense that I have returned to my body in perfect health, my physical form relaxed and vibrant with life.

The birds are singing loudly now. Soror Macha and I talk ourselves into earthly awareness.

"I cry tears of joy."

Our words, descriptions, weaving together a memory of this time, bringing back these insights and attempting to fix some tiny proportion of them into memory.

Wisdom is here but the first thing I manage to say aloud is simply, "Wow – fuck, shit!"

I am weeping. My nose is streaming. I have been reborn.

The Wiring under the Board

(A paper given at Techgnosis Symposium organised by Strange Attractor, November 2004.)

It's a great opportunity to talk to you wonderful people, and an honour to be asked to speak at an event that celebrates the re-issue of Erik's book.

Techgnosis isn't only about computers but it is the technologies of information that form the landscape of much of Erik's book. Now I'm sure many of us here tonight are confirmed computer users. Certainly, when Mark Pilkington asked me to speak his request came in the form of an email. In due course I checked out the *Strange Attractor* web page and sent it on to a number of my mates to alert them to this evening's fun. When I needed directions here tonight I consulted the internet and even made a brief series of searches to find out a bit more about where I was going. The Elephant and Castle eh? Where occultist and artist AOS used to hang out...

This talk itself was composed from a series of random quotes and jottings on a computer and has only very recently found its way into a three dimensional 'hard copy' form.

The electronic dance of digital data is an evocative, magickal process. And Erik ably demonstrates in his book that the ghost is very much in the computerised machine.

The occultist and author Ramsey Dukes described the IT industry as a demon, a spirit, certainly a view in accord with *Techgnosis*. Ramsey points out that the spirit of the IT industry (indeed any spirit) will seek to thrive and persist and to do so will create stories, ideas, 'memes' to propagate – to spawn, and of course some of these reproductive methods involve tricks...

Dukes writes;

"Among the many ludicrous myths put about by technologies in their struggle for survival there is the following:

Information technology is creating absolutely unbelievable new possibilities for instantaneous communication, information retrieval and processing. The problem is that most people are too rigid in their thinking to grasp this incredible opportunity. The real hope lies with the next generation, because only children seem able to cope with this explosion in human potential.

What a load of old cobblers! The reason that most people resist computerisation and networked communications is not because it is so mind-boggling but because it is such absolute and utterly useless crap. The fact that children (who know no better) can tolerate such rubbish is wide open to alternative interpretations."

He goes on:

"In the 50s we turned to Dan Dare in *The Eagle* comic strip who could speak to his wrist TV and be in immediate contact with any of his crew, anywhere. Far from gasping with incredulity…we grew up believing that instant walkie talkie video communications were coming any day. Forty years on we are still waiting. The IT industry has failed to deliver and it is now generating these ludicrous myths about human resistance to novelty as a smokescreen to hide its own incompetence.

The IT industry is not the leading edge of human imagination. It is a tired old windbag. I propose bulldozing the entire mob of them into a mass grave with nothing on the headstone except their own inane epitaph of non-communication: "C: BAD COMMAND OR FILENAME".

Meanwhile our expectation turns to the genetic engineers …what I want is to be born with a small benign tumour in my brain, one which is a wireless link to a worldwide communications network…one with enough bandwidth to deliver the full sensory experience."

Of course Dukes is criticising the spirit of information technology in its own terms: how much worse it gets if we look at the real world inhabited by the 'virtual domain'. While today's kids in the so-called developed world are hungry for the latest 3G mobile, the kids in the Congo get their homes torched in a civil war, the flames of which are fanned by our desire for raw materials that feed our information revolution.

But I'd like to stay within the techno mythology itself and focus specifically on the internet. Since Ramsey wrote his scathing attack in the 90s things have perhaps improved in terms of the functionality of the net. But what is the context and content of this new technological triumph?

Founding figure of the internet Tim Berners-Lee envisaged the World Wide Web as an organic expanse of collaboration, but also worries about whether it will 'allow cranks and nut cases to find in the world 20 or 30 other cranks and nut cases who are absolutely convinced of the same things. Allow them to set up filters around themselves... and develop a pothole of culture out of which they can't climb.'"

Many social commentators have been able to alert us to a number of the Nazi millennialist crazies out there on the digital highway, cheerfully swapping their own local prejudices for a global vision of nastiness. And of course, as governments are fond of reminding us, the net is crawling with paedophile terrorist drug pushers stalking the electronic underground, even as we blithely do our shopping in the bright shiny mall of Amazon and an.nother dot com.

We are all beginning to see how the internet can become a tool for observation and monitoring. As an example, both mega-corporations and governments want to see a cashless economy. Ostensibly, this is to fight the 'war on terror' but really we all know it's about developing the ultimate electronic point of sale system, where every turn of the customer's life cycle can be traced. Money, that most mythic and vital of forces, can be monitored and suspicious transactions can be flagged, escalated and investigated more effectively than ever before. Oh yes, and in the ultimate double bluff we are told that **we** are the watchers watching the watchmen. Democracy is become the gaoler of the people. Perhaps this process is hardly surprising, given the cold war origins of this technology. At the end of the 20th century it may be that it was Star Trek fans that breathed delight into the content of the burgeoning net, but the origins of the system were firmly framed through the consciousness of the US military.

We're increasingly seeing attempts to create an informational background to our lives, especially through technologies such as mobile phones. But even these developments are worlds away from William Gibson's vision of cyberspace: "A consensual hallucination...a graphic representation of data abstracted from the banks of every computer in the human system...lines of light ranged in the non-space of the mind."

Movement through data - that's what we'd really like. Perhaps part of the problem with the net is the interface as Ramsey suggests – we want the "full sensory experience". To be embodied in it. The conceptualisation of the internet is that of movement, location, surfing, visiting, we travel without moving. And at present our model of what this would mean is VR.

But has the industry delivered? No – in fact what Terry Pratchett said to me still holds true:

'Virtual reality is like having a ZX spectrum stuck on your head, while the kids in the real reality steal the hubcaps off your car.'

Of course most VR is aimed at military applications, but occasionally some escapes into other domains.

For instance, a Dr Hoffman of Seattle is in the process of developing a treatment programme for the survivors of the 9/11 attacks on the World Trade Centre. He's built a virtual reality programme that is a simulation of the events of 9/11 designed to de-sensitise the patient to the events of that day.

He says - "Virtual 'exposure' therapy allows access to the event a step at a time, starting with getting up on the morning of September 11th and gradually working up to the most disturbing events of the memory. It is a controlled way of eliciting and processing the memories."

One patient overcame her sense of guilt at running away from the scene and failing to help others who subsequently died. Virtual reality exposure therapy has helped return a sense of calm and acceptance to her life - oh well that's okay then isn't it?

So VR does work, after a fashion. The human brain is so forgiving and clever that we are prepared to forgive the shite pixilated graphics and go with it.

What we really want is something 'better than life'. The point about the artificial reality as represented by the movie *The Matrix* is that the VR world looks like the real world here - not like the Technicolor universe of the 1992 film *The Lawnmower Man*. *The Matrix* captures perfectly the idea that beneath the apparent world there is a 'something' - when we look at that cathode ray tube green code, falling like leaves, we are seeing a slice through the Tao - a symbolic representation of the ground of being.

But perhaps a far more embodying form of VR is already within our grasp, and indeed has represented a technical achievement that was accomplished millennia ago - what I'm referring to here is the art of using drugs to radically alter awareness.

Drugs are an already extant key to the world of the Imagination, the rich background information processing of mind - as I explained in my book *Pharmakon*.

Substances such as psychedelics allow us to turn down the brightness of the ego - to create a situation in which our usual frames of references are altered. And as the sun of ego reduces in brilliance so we see the stars at noon - the parallel processing background of our own mental architecture.

What Gibson yearns for in his cyberspace, Terence McKenna located in the depths of the DMT trance where 'meaning is beheld' and we see not only the form of information but begin to develop a sense of 'the writing under the board'.

So what am I saying - the web is bad but drugs are good? That drugs emerge from the realm of nature and are ok, whereas the artificial culture of the net is human and harmful? Or perhaps that all we need to do is down tools on the digital domain and start munching the mushrooms?

No - what I'm saying is that both these things, both these technologies – drugs and computers - (and perhaps all technologies) are pharmakons - they are both a medicine and a poison. And whilst we can fling simplistic criticisms about information technology about, this betokens an impoverished engagement with these spirits.

For these things, these technologies are spirits, entities like you and I and as complex in their behaviour as we are – computers and drugs are special arrangements of matter that are enchanted.

No technology, whether it is the use of psychedelics or the internet, springs from a purely utilitarian world but rather is birthed by and into the mythic structures of our culture.

And this is happening all around us, and is a process that, in my opinion, Erik's book is all about - that is the re-enchantment of the world, or perhaps not re-enchantment but rather a reminder of the fact that we live in an inherently enchanted, magickal, mythic universe.

Those simplistic dualisms of nature and culture, subject and object, good and bad begin to collapse when we are faced with any cultural creation that has sufficient complexity to have developed its own spirit. Our technologies are tricksters (as Ramsey points out when describing how they seek to perpetuate themselves) and that is why it is Thoth, Thrice Great Hermes, Mercury that is the god of physicians, magickians, technicians and tricksters.

So the same accusations I have levelled against information technology can also be applied to the world of drugs. They are also able to destroy as well as liberate. Our society has hatched huge slave trade networks to keep the drugs flowing, and revenue from drug sales to the poor and hopeless feeds a variety of monsters. The happy pills, of whatever sort, lull us into a complicit, comfortably numb state, in which even TV seems interesting.

Drugs fail to live up to their own hype as often as the IT industry sells us empty promises. Ibogaine isn't a one-size fits all painless remover of addictions. LSD doesn't turn anyone who takes it into a Bodisattva and the MDMA hasn't ushered in an era of world peace.

The Cartesian, or perhaps Gnostic, divisions that infest our culture emerge, that Erik explores in Techgnosis also exist in the discourses of drugs.

Psychedelic aficionados debate whether 'natural' drugs are preferable to 'artificial' preparations. But to adopt this sort of position is to miss the point, to have failed to have glimpsed 'the wiring under the board'.

My own view on the natural/artificial drugs debate was expressed eloquently by a speaker at the recent UK Exploring Consciousness conference who said that Alexander Shulgin was as much a product of nature as anything else and so, by extension, were the fabulous array of materials he had created. And this kind of logic is what we need when engaging with any technology, a logic where we truly appreciate the Hermetic vision that all things are connected. We need to look for approaches that unpick the superficial dichotomies of perception and seek connections. Not that we should reject any attempt at categorisation and definition, but we must remain mindful that any definition is contingent, subject to change and that perhaps nothing is true and everything is possible.

Social commentators like Erik are seeking to understand the zeitgeist, the underlying mythic structures of culture. Such people peer beneath simplistic assumptions, easy prejudices and divisions. We need people who can do this, who can explore without damming or deifying the territory of their explorations. So the simplistic "the internet was invented by the military and is therefore ideologically always going to be a bad thing" can be challenged, thrown into question. Just as Erik has challenged the assumption that magick has been replaced by science by saying, hold on it's a lot more complicated than that.

This separation of science and technology from magick and art - healing this divide is one of the central shamanic tasks of our age and this is important. This refusal to see things in terms of this or that, of simple dualisms of good and bad, but rather to learn to chart a course through shifting layers of meanings and interpretation is essential. Because it is through this process that we can become something of what we might call the contemporary Renaissance man and woman. Such a person is one who rejects the simplistic assumptions of capitalism vs. anarchism or art vs. science. Such an intelligent generalist, of the type that Erik represents, would probably agree with Robert Heinlein:

"A human being should be able to change a diaper, plan an invasion, butcher a hog, design a building, conn a ship, write a sonnet, balance accounts, build a wall, set a bone, comfort the dying, take orders, give orders, cooperate, act alone, solve an equation, analyze a new problem, pitch manure, program a computer, cook a tasty meal, fight efficiently, die gallantly. Specialization is for insects."

Such a breadth of skills is essential when we plunge and plug into technologies such as drugs and the use of computers. Our refusal to accept superficial dualisms in attempting to develop wider vistas of understanding is critical, because if we look up from our narrow worldview who knows what we might see?

One example of a person who looked up is the story of a man called Mordechai Vanunu. Recently re-arrested, Vanunu was a subordinate technician at a nuclear plant when he blew the whistle on Israel's clandestine nuclear weapons programme. He was abducted from Italy to Israel and was sentenced as a spy to eighteen years in prison. The first eleven and a half years, were spent in solitary confinement, where he wrote this:

I am the clerk, the technician, the mechanic, the driver.

They said, do this, do that, don't look left or right,

don't read the text. Don't look at the whole machine. You

are only responsible for this one bolt. For this one rubber-stamp.

This is your only concern. Don't bother with what is above you.

Don't try to think for us. Go on, drive. Keep going. On, on.

So how do we stop systems – whether they are information technologies, pharmaceutical technologies, political or religious ideologies - turning us into the blind cogs in the machine? I think the answer is that we need attempts at 'the big picture' and more than that we need expeditions into the wiring under the board. We need people like Ramsey Dukes who can educate us to the way systems function as entities, as spirits, and help us learn to negotiate with these things. We need people like Erik Davis who can link together worlds, who can bring us face to face with the zeitgeist, the archetypal matrix that functions under consciousness, beneath the surface of culture. For it is by us seeking these occult, these hidden, connections between objects in the world that we can challenge hegemony and enrich and enchant our worlds.

Armageddon, Utopia and Us.

(A Second World War siren sounds across the Sussex landscape. This announced the beginning of this talk and practical tai chi workshop at the Anderida Grove Druid camp.)

What I'd like to do is set the scene with a little talk and then to get on with some practical magickal work. As a preface to the practical section of this workshop, I need to tell you that we'll be doing some physical breathing exercises – so please make sure you are warm and comfortable.

The end of the world is nigh – can't we see it all around us? Let's contemplate for a moment a sequence of images, the detonation of a nuclear device at Nagasaki, the storming of the school in Beslan, the collapse of the twin towers.

But this isn't just in the human world of immediate artificially manufactured conflict; the Indian ocean Tsunami, the flood waters pushed by a gigantic hurricane inundating New Orleans. These aren't just isolated events of terror or natural disaster.

Armageddon is begun.

Now I'm not brushing aside the tragedy, the sadness and horror of many of these events. In fact, in some ways I want to make us all appreciate them in themselves even more directly. Because I'd like us to consider that the way I have presented these things – as elements in the dawning Apocalypse, the end of the world, robs them of their meaning in themselves because they become just pieces of a much larger story. And that story is one called Eschatology.

Eschatology literally means the study of the eschaton, the times of the end, 'last things', or 'end times.' In Zoroastrianism, Christianity, Rastafari, and in Norse pagan theology, eschatology is a theology concerning the end of the world, as predicted in the prophecies of these faiths, and as recorded in their sacred texts. It can also be the study of general afterlife concepts of other religions, especially the western monotheistic faiths. In this broader sense, eschatology can refer to the Messiah, a messianic era, the afterlife and the soul in religions which have such beliefs.

The word is derived from Greek *eskhatos* meaning last, furthest, remote, with the root ex — "out of".

As far as is known, Zoroastrianism, by 500 B.C, had a fully developed concept of the end of the world as being devoured by fire, and is thus the oldest known eschatology.

Now Pagans also have eschatological ideas in some of their beliefs. The idea that a New Age is dawning, the Age of Aquarius or whatever is prevalent in New Age thought, appears in various forms in Paganism.

Here is the grandfather of modern Paganism Aleister Crowley commenting on what he called the coming Aeon of Horus.

"He rules the present period of 2,000 years beginning in 1904. Everywhere his government is taking root. Observe

for yourselves the decay of the sense of sin, the growth of innocence and irresponsibility, the strange modifications of

the reproductive instinct with a tendency to become bi-sexual or epicene, the childlike confidence in progress combined

with nightmare fear of catastrophe, against which we are yet half unwilling to take precautions.

Consider the outcrop of dictatorships, only possible when moral growth is in its earliest stages, and the prevalence of infantile cults like Communism, Fascism, Pacifism, Health Crazes, Occultism in nearly all its forms, religions sentimentalized to the point of practical extinction.

Consider the popularity of the cinema, the wireless, the football pools and guessing competitions, all devices for soothing fractious infants, no seed of purpose in them.

Consider sport, the babyish enthusiasms and rages which it excites, whole nations disturbed by disputes between boys.

We are children."

Now of course it's not all gloom – for some people Armageddon is what we really need, it may be hard and sure some people will be causalities but this is an inevitable process. If entering the new age is just like growing up then there are bound to be growing pains, difficulties, dangers. But imagine how fabulous the new age could be, a utopia that blends the best of ancient wisdom and modern technology. The process might be driven by forces as inexorable as evolution towards some kind of shift in awareness, a 100th monkey, Aquarian conspiracy type revolution, who knows what might happen. We might discover all manner of better, more holistic, ways to live together, or who knows we might even completely change our vibrational level and become beings of pure energy…

Of course this is utopia – the perfect, perfected world. Now perhaps here at this camp designed to explore the three worlds we have a model. There is this world, then there is the underworld - the place of the apocalypse, the dead, chaos, and finally there is utopia, the gods, order, the upperworld.

Or to put it more simply there is here, heaven and hell.

Well, yes, this is a myth and a popular one at that, a popular way of imagining the universe. But is it what we want? What we need? I don't think so.

The apocalypse and utopia are powerful mythic structures, powerful archetypes but I think at this camp we can, and should, start to challenge these psychic structures. Because this is part of what transformation, what magick, is about. It's about challenging and shaking things up, about discovering new ways to perceive the world and new ways of being in it.

So let's begin to pick holes in our perceptions of these two archetypes.

The term Utopia is derived from a book written in 1515 by Thomas More. In the book a fictional traveller describes the political arrangements of an imaginary island nation named Utopia (a play on the Greek ou-topos, meaning "no place", and eu-topos, meaning "good place"). More contrasts the contentious social life of Christian European states with the perfectly orderly and reasonable social arrangements of the non-Christian Utopia, where private property does not exist and an almost complete religious toleration is practiced. Many commentators have pointed out that Karl Marx's later vision of the ideal communist state strongly resembles More's Utopia.

His own attitude towards the arrangements he describes in the book is the subject of much debate.

And I'm sure we can all image that one person's utopia is another person's dystopia – or hell.

Part of the problem is that whoever creates the utopia tends to want to rule the roost. For example, in Plato's utopia, his Republic, he assumes that philosophers should be kings.

And even if we take concepts like truth, justice, compromise – things I think most of us would say are basically good things, and try to apply them as absolute principles in a utopian vision, we soon run into problems.

For instance in the story *Harrison Bergernon* Kurt Vonnegut describes a future society where equality is strictly enforced, often through the introduction of deliberate technological handicap. Those with excellent eyesight are compelled to wear glasses to distort their vision, the strong are connected to mechanisms that limit their mobility and people with high intelligence are subject to piercing sounds sent to their brains every few seconds to disturb their train of thought.

And outside of the Brave New Worlds of fiction we have examples from ethnography of how societies that we might take as utopian can actually behave. My favourite example of this is the Waorani people. They live in South America, and their society is ecologically sustainable and completely egalitarian. They have no chiefs; a Wao leader may emerge for a specific act, but each person remains intensely independent. Until the 1950s this culture remained untouched by the western world. But now Christianity, anthropology and technology have arrived. And has this improved the lot of these people – the answer in one word is yes!

You see the Waorani people are extremely violent. In the Amazon where they live, they dwell on the hilltops, avoiding the flooded river valleys, they do not swim and linguistic evidence suggests their culture has been isolated for many generations from neighbouring tribes. Cut off from the outside world they lived in almost constant fear and suspicion. The

directions, we're putting ourselves in the centre of the world, all worlds, in the heartwood of Yggdrasil.

So what methods are available for us to approach this task? One possibility is to examine the techniques developed within Taoism. Now Taoism has a lot in common with modern neo-paganism. It draws inspiration from animal forms (having as it does its roots in Asian shamanism), it rejoices in, rather than rejects, the world, and has a rich tradition of magickal practices. Taoism includes a number of approaches that have been described as alchemical. The alchemy of Taoism seeks to return to the flexibility and openness of youth but with the wisdom and wide experience of age. Taoism does not seek to create a harmonious culture through conscious planning and practice (incidentally the USA is an example of a consciously planned utopian culture based on liberty and the pursuit of happiness, and it is arguably one of the most violent and unjust nations on earth). Instead it invites us to cultivate the nourishing power of universe to move through us. The assumption is that right action flows from being connected to the well spring of the Tao. And it's not that we should not seek to make moral choices about the world, that we shouldn't act – I'm not for example suggesting that the ethnic cleansing in Bosnia was somehow 'natural' or simply part of the process of the universe that should not have been opposed. But what I am suggesting is that the internalised forces, psychic structures such as utopia and Armageddon can be things we all carry around within us, and that because of history, media, culture and our own internal processes we can get stuck with them. Like muscles that get used to moving in a certain habitual pattern, we become restricted.

Although the Taoist tradition includes magick sigils, gestures, potions, ceremonies and all the rest, one of its most enduring and popular approaches is through the body, through practices such as chi gong, and martial arts such as tai chi.

Think about it the same way that you do about the idea of opening the chakras or other energy centres in your organism. Think about it the way NLP (Neuro-linguistic programming)suggests that memories and behaviours get anchored into movements and the very way we hold our bodies. What we're doing here is undoing ourselves.

You see to be the *axis mundi*, to act in the world and not to get trapped in the myths of utopia or Apocalypse (or indeed any other 'trip') what the Taoists suggest is that one needs to flow. To move, to be open. So rather than doing some kind of ritual practice I'm going to suggest that we do some body work. The aim of this is that we are going to open ourselves out, to find the void, the spaces in our bodies and in our minds. The central point of now, the middle pillar that links all three worlds. We become hollow, like the stem of a bamboo (or perhaps an elder tree!) to let the magick, the transformation flow through us.

Now to let this flow take place what we need to do is not do. That is, relax, enjoy, have fun; so as we go through this set of exercises, do them gently. No gritted teeth please, if your mind wanders, as it will, gently come back to the practice. What you're doing is opening yourself up, becoming present in your body here and now. And don't panic if your brain doesn't think anything is happening, that doesn't mean your body isn't having a great time. We've got an action packed time ahead of us at this camp and by doing this bodywork we're making a space in our physical forms, making an alchemical transformation so that the three worlds are here and now.

And this is where we get to the practical bit.

Begin by loosening up.

Shaking.

Stepping.

Swinging the arms.

Shoulder rolling.

Weeping willow stretch.

Head tapping, ears popping etc.

Grand circles.

Breathing while moving arms up and down.

Waving hands in clouds.

Standing posture, relax all tension, thoughts and feelings – relax and shake.

Take these exercises and do your own thing.

Ecstasy of the Spirit, Joy on Earth

(A Working for Camp Chaos 2006.)

Background

Modern neo-pagan witchcraft has become an acceptable religion. It has begun, in many parts of the English speaking world, to be an unusual although acceptable religious practice. The label Pagan is now rarely used in a negative context by mainstream media.

The Aim

From this increasingly secure position neopaganism (of which Wicca is one of the earliest manifestations) can seek to make demands of wider culture. This is already happening in that Pagans are seeking, and often getting, 'their rights' in a number of contexts (prison, hospital, holiday entitlements etc). My suggestion is that Paganism is one of the approaches that might help breakdown the defences of what Jonathan Ott calls the "Phamacratic Inquisition."

In essence Paganism, especially witchcraft, is a cult of ecstasy. The religious right to use herbs, medicines, entheogens is a key religious freedom. Religion is perhaps one of the few stalking horses of sufficient power to breach the defences of the Inquisition. Successful attempts to breach these defences have already come from ayahuasca users and the Native American Church.

By using the system of Alexandrian/Gardnarian Wicca in this ceremony we are attempting to situate the influence of the spell in the style of praxis that underlies most contemporary witchcraft (and indeed more widely throughout neopaganism). Also this tradition does contain, even if as something of a recessive meme, the notion of its being a cult of ecstasy. This meme is fully embedded in many sections of The Charge, particularly in those elements derived from Crowley.

The process

The process for the ritual will be a fairly standard Gardnarian/Alexandrian circle casting and invocation of the Goddess. The cakes and wine will be consecrated in the usual way. This will include a sacrament. The idea is to connect the work of people using sacraments directly with the egregore of modern Paganism to increase the demand for actual pharmacologically generated ecstasy. A sigil has been selected that combines the eight rayed star of the chaos with the triangle+pentagram of Wicca and the symbol of the eight fold wheel (of the year and paths of power). This will be placed on a drum which we hope to keep going all night.

Criteria for success
This will be observed in the form of an increasing desire by Pagans to be permitted to make use of scared medicines in their worship. This desire will exert a pressure on existing drug laws and lead to changes in legislation.

Rubric

Preparation.

Salt and water are available on the altar. A wand and athame are present. Lights are set at each of the four directions. NB the altar is (now) in metaphysical North.

Officers are selected for each part of the rite. A pentacle holding the sacrament is present, as is wine. The drum with the sigil on it is present, as is a broom. Incense is lit. The Book of Shadows containing The Charge is also available.

Before the rite begins Officers are chosen (roles: Broom, Salt & Water, Incense, Fire, Watchtowers & Drum)

All stand as witches (ie skyclad and alternately male/female).

Praxis

1. Officer sweeps circle with broom.

2. Cast circle – this is done with the athame/sword by the High Priest.

"I conjure thee, O Circle of Power, that thou beest
    a boundary between the world of men and the realms of
the Mighty Ones;
    a meeting place of love and joy and truth;
    a shield against all wickedness and evil;

a rampart and protection that shall preserve and contain
the power that we raise within thee.
Wherefore do I bless thee, and consecrate thee,

3. The salt and water are consecrated – the High Priest and High Priestess kneel before the altar. The High Priest holds the water and the High Priestess draws a pentagram over it (invoking earth pentagrams are used throughout the ritual) and says:

"I exorcise thee, O creature of Water, that thou cast out from Thee all the impurities and uncleannesses of the Spirits of the World of Phantasm, wherefore do I exorcise thee in the most sacred names of Aradia and Cernunnos."

The HP blesses the salt.

"Blessings be upon this creature of Salt, and let all malignity and hindrance be cast forth hencefrom, and let all good enter herein, wherefore do I bless and consecrate thee in the most sacred names of Aradia and Cernunnos."

4. The salt and water are then sprinkled around the circle by an officer. Each participant is marked on the forehead with water.

5. An officer takes the censer round the circle raising it at each direction and offering it to each person in term to breathe in.

6. Another officer takes the right altar candle round the circle offering it to the directions and each person present. As it passes each person they raise their hands up to feel the warmth of the flame.

7. The watchtowers are then called by an Officer, starting from the East.

"Ye Lords of the Watchtowers of the East, ye Lords of Air;
We do summon, stir and call you up, to witness our
    rites and guard the Circle ! and we do bid ye hail and welcome"

All: "Hail and welcome"

8. All join hands and circle deosil as the witches rune is performed:

Darksome night and shining moon,

East, then south, then west, then north,
Hearken to the witches' rune:
Here we come to call thee forth.

Earth and water, air and fire,
Wand and pentacle and sword,
Work you unto my desire,
Hearken ye unto our word.

Cords and censer, scourge and knife,
Powers of the witches blade
Waken all ye unto life,
Come ye as the charm is made.

Queen of heaven, Queen of hell,
Horned hunter of the night,
Lend your power unto my spell
And work my will by magic rite.

By all the power of land and sea,
By all the might of moon and sun,
As we do will, so mote it be:
Chant this spell, and be it done.

Eko, Eko, Azarak,
Eko, Eko, Zamilak,
Eko, Eko, Cernunnos,
Eko, Eko, Aradia.

(Repeat last verse until gnosis attained, then all fall to the floor.)

9.   Drawing Down the Moon

High Priestess stands in front of Altar, assumes Goddess position (arms crossed). High Priest, kneeling in front of her, draws pentacle on her body with Wand, invokes:

"I Invoke Thee, O mighty Mother of all life and fertility. By seed and root, by stem and bud, by leaf and flower and fruit, by Life and Love, do I invoke Thee to descend into the body of thy servant and High Priestess [name]."

10. The High Priest gives the Goddess the fivefold kiss.

The Moon having been drawn down, i.e., link established, Magus and other men give Fivefold Kiss:

(kissing feet) "Blessed be thy feet, that have brought thee in these ways";

(kissing knees) "Blessed be thy knees, that shall kneel at the sacred altar";

(kissing womb) "Blessed be thy womb, without which we would not be";

(kissing breasts) "Blessed be thy breasts, formed in beauty and in strength";

(kissing lips) "Blessed be thy lips, that shall speak the sacred names."

11. Charge

The High Priestess now reads the Charge and/or speaks words of Wisdom.

High Priest: *Listen to the Words of the Great Mother, Who was of old called among men Artemis, Astarte, Diana, Melusine, Aphrodite, Cerridwen, Dana, Arianrhod, Isis, Bride, and by many other Names.*

Whenever ye have need of anything, once in the month, and better it be when the Moon is Full, then shall ye gather in some secret place and adore the Spirit of Me, Who am Queen of All Witches. There shall ye gather, ye who are fain to learn all Magick, yet have not yet won its deepest secrets: to these will I teach things that are yet unknown.

And ye shall be free from slavery; and as a sign that ye be really free, ye shall be naked in your rites. And ye shall dance, sing, feast, make music and love, all in My Praise. For Mine is the Ecstasy of the Spirit, and Mine also is Joy on Earth, for My Law is Love unto all beings.

Keep pure your Highest Ideal; strive ever toward it; let naught stop you or turn you aside. For Mine is the Secret Door which opens upon the Land of Youth; and Mine is the Cup of the Wine of Life, and the Cauldron of Cerridwen, which is the Holy Grail of Immortality.

I am the Gracious Goddess, Who gives the Gift of Joy unto the heart of man: on Earth, I give the Knowledge of the Spirit Eternal; and beyond death, I give peace, and freedom, and reunion with those who have gone before. Nor do I demand sacrifice, for behold: I am the Mother of All Living, and My Love is poured out upon the Earth.

High Priest: *Hear ye the Words of the Star Goddess: She in the Dust of Whose Feet are the Hosts of Heaven, Whose Body encircleth the Universe.*

I, Who am the Beauty of the Green Earth, and the White Moon amongst the Stars, and the Mystery of the Waters, and the Desire of the heart of man, I call unto thy soul: "Arise! And come unto Me!"

For I am the Soul of Nature, Who giveth Life to the Universe: from Me all things proceed, and unto Me all things must return. And before My Face, which is beloved of gods and men, thine innermost Divine Self shall be enfolded in the Rapture of the Infinite.

Let My Worship be within the heart that rejoiceth, for behold: all acts of love and pleasure are my rituals. And therefore let there be beauty and strength, power and compassion, honour and humility, mirth and reverence within you.

And thou who thinkest to seek for Me, know thy seeking and yearning shall avail thee not, unless thou knowest the Mystery: that if that which thou seekest thou findest not within thee, thou wilt never find it without thee.

For behold, I have been with thee from the beginning; and I am That which is attained at the end of Desire.

12. Cakes and Wine

High Priest kneels holding the cup.

High Priestess, holding Athame between palms, places point in cup.

High Priest: "As the Athame is the Male, so the Cup is the female; so, conjoined, they bring blessedness."

High Priestess lays aside Athame, takes Cup in both hands, drinks and gives drink.

High Priest Holds Pentacle to High Priestess, who blesses with Athame, then eats and gives to eat.

An officer begins to drum

All: "Ecstasy of the Spirit, Joy on Earth!"

Laughter, dancing and frolics begin…

Closing.

13. Later, the watchtowers are thanked (deosil):

"Ye Lords of the Watchtowers of the East, ye Lords of Air; We thank for attending our rite and now we bid you hail and farewell".

All: "Hail and farewell"

The Fourth Path

Drugs, Entheogens and modern Paganism

(An article printed in the Pagan Federation journal Pagan Dawn.)

Let's consider for a moment some archetypal images of magic, a series of icons that are so well known that they have common currency both within and outside of paganism.

The first is the witch. There she stands into the shadowy darkness at the edge of the wild wood. Dressed in black, perhaps young and enchanting, perhaps a decaying aged crone. In either form we know what she is doing. She bends over a huge cauldron from which clouds of strangely coloured steam rise; she throws a handful of rare and powerful herbs into the brew and chants her spell.

Here is another. The alchemist, the bearded mage who has spent his life on a quest for that most magical of materials; the philosopher's stone. In a laboratory bristling with curiously shaped instruments of glass and metal, he gazes intently at the contents of a retort on his workbench. A gentle flame below it is agitating the mysterious fluid contained within. Perhaps this time he will have done it, perhaps this time he will be able to transmute base lead into spiritual gold...

And one more image; far away in the depths of the Amazon basin the members of the tribe are chanting. A young man, his body painted with intricate images of grids, spirals and stylised animals approaches the shaman. The shaman raises a pipe made from the long hollow bones of the harpy eagle. The young initiate slides the end of the pipe into his nostril and murmurs a final prayer to the ancestors. The shaman shakes a rattle to banish any evil spirits and blows the magical powder through the pipe and into the young man.

I expect you've guessed the connection. Although there are undoubtedly differences between the forms of spiritual or occult practice I've given in my examples they all make use of magical substances. Moreover these substances are crucial parts of their practice. Where would the witch be without her herbs? Where the alchemist without his powders and solvents? Where the shaman without their power plants?

The use of chemicals, whether we describe them as drugs, psychoactives, plant allies or whatever is deeply rooted in the imagery of ancient paganism. But this isn't an anachronistic practice we talking about because the use of magical herbs is something that is also very much part of modern paganism.

Virtually all cultures, both ancient and modern, make use of sacred plants and special magical substances. Sometimes these things function on the symbolic level; the battle between the brothers of Oak and Holly, for instance, in the modern pagan wheel of the year. But often our most powerful and most celebrated sacred substances are those that actually do things to our biochemistry. These are substances that can quite literally change our minds. Alcohol, for example, is enshrined in myths as diverse as those of Dionysus, John Barleycorn and Jesus. An awareness of, and indeed the use of, these sacred substances was certainly there at the beginning of modern paganism. Dion Fortune in *The Mystical Qabalah* describes how various drugs can be linked to the sephira of the Tree of Life. Aleister Crowley experimented with a wide variety of drugs as part of his magick (and he wasn't alone in doing so). Gerald Gardner, too, enshrined the use of drugs as one of the techniques of changing consciousness in Wicca. The text below appears in Gardner's 1953 version of *The Book of Shadows* as the "Eightfold Path or Ways to the Centre", the entry for the fourth path says:

4. *Incense, Drugs, Wine, etc., whatever is used to release the Spirit.*

Of course part of the impetus of modern paganism also comes from the cultural revolutions of the 1960s and 1970s. Changes in sexual morality, technology and economics were both fuelled by, and reflected in, the increasing availability of magical substances. The most important of these was LSD. Naturally lots of people, particularly the US government (who had initially hoped to use LSD as a weapon) were rather distressed that this substance was (it seemed) likely to lead to more and more people quitting university, dodging military service in Vietnam and getting involved in the process of self-discovery. As the later part of the twentieth century progressed two things happened. First, more and more magical substances became available to a wider and wider audience (especially in the English speaking world) and secondly more and more laws were created, reaching their illogical conclusion in the 'War on Drugs'.

Modern paganism was steadily growing through this time, fed by the streams of insight and energy that the use of magical substances generated. The interest in eastern thought, alternative religion and ecology was galvanised by the LSD revolution. Meanwhile people interested in such things were just beginning to discover that in our very own back yard we had psychedelic mushrooms growing and a number of other psychedelic plants. Having already read Carlos Castaneda's tales of the shaman Don Juan using datura and mescaline, the fact that we had our own indigenous power plants seemed too good to be true. Later the spontaneous shamanism of MDMA use, which emerged in the 'rave culture' of the late 1980s and early 1990s, created a cultural hunger for understanding about trance states. Hybrids like technopaganism developed and towards the end of the 1990s, as well as more direct contact between industrialised cultures and tribal shamanic practitioners. The rising interest in shamanism and tribal cultures brought Sioux tobacco ceremonies and Amazonian *ayahuasceros* (Amazonian healers using the powerful drugs harmala and DMT) to the shores of the UK.

Of course, over the last 100 and particularly the last 50 years western culture has projected a tremendous amount of fear onto the use of drugs. Why is this, and what has been the effect?

I believe that the main reason that a wide variety of governments and political ideologies find the use of magical substances repellent is, at root, very simple; it is because they fear ecstasy. Both communist and consumer capitalist, right and left wing governments have attempted to stop people using drugs with increasingly punitive legislation with very little success. Indeed as the experiment of alcohol prohibition in the USA made clear, making a drug illegal only serves to provide a ready made commodity for organised crime and criminalise the harmless consumption of the majority of users. The tactic of banning substance X, apparently because of perceived health risks (such as addictive behaviour) does not work in eliminating that substance from a culture.

Naturally when pagans have written about drugs are they aware of the problems of addiction. Gardner, for instance, in the 1953 entry on the fourth path in *The Book of Shadows* says:

One must be very careful about this *[ie the use of drugs]*. Incense is usually harmless, but you must be careful. If it has bad after-effects, reduce the amount used, or the duration of the time it is inhaled. Drugs are very dangerous if taken to excess, but it must be remembered that there are drugs that are absolutely harmless, though people talk of them with bated breath...

Of course drugs can be dangerous taken in excess. As indeed can egg and chips, or water, or indeed anything else. But we don't teach our children not to gorge themselves sick on chocolate biscuits by locking the biscuit barrel and throwing away the key. We should be aiming at creating examples of intelligent use rather than adopting a prohibitionist 'thou shalt not' approach.

The cultural fear of ecstasy, whether it is generated by fasting, chanting, dancing or drugs isn't hard to understand in cultures (such as ours) that prize control and order. But for pagans things can be somewhat different. For many of us trance states, alterations in consciousness and awareness are what our traditions are all about. From the seething practices of Norse seidhr to the mythic drama of Druid group ceremony – the aim is the same, to change the way our minds work, to discover new relationships between self and other, and perhaps to become caught up in the ecstatic power of the gods. Successfully including these states within a culture can be difficult, but as many tribal societies demonstrate it is far from impossible. Part of the process of accommodating the ecstatic experience within our culture comes from returning to an understanding of the use of sacred substances as part of religious practice. To this end the term *entheogen* was coined in 1979 by a group of ethnobotanists and scholars of mythology.

An entheogen, in the strictest sense, is a psychoactive substance (most often some plant matter with hallucinogenic effects) that occasions an enlightening spiritual or mystical experience within a religious context. The word entheogen is derived from two Ancient Greek words. *Entheos* literally means "god (theos) within", more freely translated "inspired". The Greeks used it as a term of praise for poets and other artists.

Genesthai means, "to cause to be" or *becoming*. So an entheogen is "that which causes God (or godly inspiration) to be within a person".

It is with this definition in mind that an increasing number of groups are demanding that their use of entheogens as part of their religion be respected. Groups such as the Native American Church are permitted to use the mescaline rich peyote cactus in their rituals. A case in 2001 confirmed the right of the Santo Daime Church (whose rituals derive from a fusion of Catholic Christianity and South American paganism) to possess and use ayahuasca. The case of ayahuasca is a perfect example. The sacred substance itself is a powerful vision-inducing tea manufactured in South America. It has a very well established pedigree having been used by shaman from many cultures for perhaps many thousands of years. Its effectiveness arises because it contains DMT, a substance that naturally occurs in the human body but which also (bizarrely) is a class A (UK Law) and schedule I (US law) prohibited psychoactive.

In a recent case in Holland the lack of public health risks and the emphasis that should be placed on the constitutional Freedom of Religion made the court decide in favour of the Santo Daime Church. But it's not all been straightforward. In France, the Santo Daime Church won a court case allowing them to use ayahuasca in 2005. However, they were not allowed an exception for religious purposes, but rather for the simple reason that they did not perform chemical extractions to end up with pure DMT and the plants used were not scheduled. Four months after the court victory, the common ingredients of ayahuasca as well as harmala were declared *stupéfiants*, or narcotic schedule I substances, making the tea and its ingredients illegal to use or possess. So some authorities are quite happy to move the goal posts when it suits! Most recently a decision came in Italy in 2006. A ruling found that insufficient evidence had been presented to demonstrate that the church members had broken Italian law. In all cases it has been quite clear that the Santo Daime Church are a genuine (though recent and syncretic) religion, much like modern paganism. It has also been apparent that their use of ayahuasca is under controlled ritual circumstances. The most recent victory has been by another ayahuasca using group the União do Vegetal (UDV). On 21 February 2006 the Supreme Court of the USA issued a unanimous verdict that usage of the ayahuasca tea as part of UDV religious ceremonies cannot be prosecuted by the federal government, in accordance with the Religious Freedom Restoration Act.

As well as the groups listed above there are certainly many pagans who feel that the use of entheogens has, is and should be seen as a valid part of our religious practice. Sacred substances from salvia divinorum through psychedelic mushrooms and cannabis are certainly used by a number of individuals and groups in the UK and the USA as part of their spirituality. I think that the time has come for pagans to start demanding that our right to use sacred herbs of many different types be respected. This is an important process and one, whether we use entheogens or not ourselves, which I feel we should support. Pagans, both individually and through groups such as the Pagan Federation have accomplished a remarkable amount in the last fifty years in terms of becoming accepted within society, and it's time that we begin to make it clear that there are some aspects of our religion that might call for changes in the law. And if the US Supreme Court can do it with the UDV why not the UK courts when it comes to the use of, for instance, magic mushrooms as part of pagan religion?

I'm not suggesting this path will be easy or that we will immediately get what we want, but for those of us who would like the freedom to walk the fourth path (as the Book of Shadows describes it) without interference from the police, this is something we must do. How can we begin? Well, one way would be by lending your support to one of the many prisoners of the 'War on Drugs'. One such person is Casey Hardison, an American living in the UK, who has been arrested and convicted of LSD manufacture in Britain. He is now contesting the case in the human rights court. He initially acted as his own lawyer during his case and, instead of claiming he did not commit the acts, he argued that he had a fundamental human right to engage in his chosen entheogenic religion. The court rejected the argument and he was sentenced to 20 years in prison in 2005. This is an astonishingly harsh sentence. If Casey had committed murder he would have probably faired better! Let's be clear. We're not talking about forlorn kids on heroin or crack crazed hoodlums here; this is about the responsible use of sacred substances in a religious context. Casey has submitted the human rights arguments simultaneously to the European Court of Human Rights and to the United Kingdom Court of Appeal directly challenging the drug laws as an affront to free thought, therapeutic choice and free religion.

Pagans might also wish to support one of the organisations that are involved in sharing information and pressing for reform of current drug laws. I've given a few examples of such groups at the end of this article. As a pagan community, we need to make our voices heard when it comes to changes in the laws that concern the use of entheogens. And it's important to realise that we **can** make these changes in legislation. Who would have thought when Oscar Wilde was gaoled for homosexuality in 1895 that seventy-two years later homosexuality would be de-criminalised in the UK? It's time for pagans to demand back our power plants and magical elixirs. It's time, I believe, for pagans to demand our right to travel the fourth path.

Places to find out more information:
erowid.org – *an excellent library relating to the use of psychoactives.*
www.freecasey.org
erowid.org/culture/characters/hardison_casey/
hardison_casey.shtml. *and* en.wikipedia.org/wiki/
Casey_William_Hardison -
for information about Casey and his situation.
www.tdpf.org.uk - *a political pressure group campaigning for change in current drug legislation.*
www.lifeline.org.uk - *working to relieve poverty, sickness and distress among those affected by addiction to drugs of any kind, and to educate the public on matters relating to drug misuse.*
santodaime.org – *information on the Santo Daime Church.*
www.udv.org.br/english/index.html – *information on the União do Vegetal (UDV).*
www.nativeamericanchurch.com – *information about the Native American Church.*

Permaculture, politics paganism

(*A lecture given at the winter assembly of the Order of Bards, Ovates and Druids in Glastonbury, Somerset.*)

So, the state of the world. Well folks, you don't need me to tell you that things are looking pretty bad. The sea level is up, the stock market is down. Our species is contributing to the extermination of hundreds of other life forms on the planet. Between ourselves we have a series of apparently irreconcilable differences that we are prepared to take murderous action over. The spectre of terrorism hangs like a jumbo jet over the polluted and dehumanising metropolis of early 21st century society.

What we need are ideas, some solutions, and we need them yesterday. And to quote the late, great, Terence McKenna what we need are middle size ideas. Not ideas that are so vast and ineffable that they can only be approached through states of mystical illumination, nor yet do we need the kind of tiny insights into the universe of the 'Hey, have you ever noticed how your little finger perfectly fits inside your nostril?' type. We need, if we are going to save, to heal, to empower our species, ideas that live in the middle ground of practical experience and realpolitik.

There are lots of tactics that one might use, lots of approaches. The one that I've encountered that helps me in addressing issues of social justice and ecological issues is known as permaculture.

So what is permaculture? Permaculture is a design system, which aims to create sustainable human habitats by following nature's patterns.

The word 'permaculture', coined by Australians Bill Mollison and David Holmgren during the 1970s, is a contraction of permanent agriculture as well as permanent culture.

Here is a lovely definition I discovered on the internet:

"Permaculture can best be described as a moral and ethical design system applicable to food production and land use, as well as community design. It seeks the creation of productive and sustainable ways of living by integrating ecology, landscape, organic gardening, architecture, agroforestry, green or ecological

151

economics, and social systems. The focus is not on these elements themselves, but rather on the relationships created among them by the way they are placed together; the whole becoming greater than the sum of its parts. Permaculture is also about careful and contemplative observation of nature and natural systems, and of recognizing universal patterns and principles, then learning to apply these 'ecological truisms' to one's own circumstances in all realms of human activity."

So, the 'careful and contemplative observation of nature'. That sounds pretty much like Druidry in action to me. And I think that there are very good reasons for suggesting that we Druids should see permaculture as an expression of our spiritual tradition.

I started reading about permaculture and getting hints about what it meant a number of years ago. But it wasn't until about five years ago that I began to study the system in earnest.

I remember the first time the guy who was the main tutor on the permaculture course I attended in Brighton took us out to the woods in Sussex and asked us to look at a tree.

'Where does it get what it needs from?' he asked us. Now one of the answers is that a tree (and indeed any living system) gets its needs met locally but it is also plugged into global systems (the atmosphere for instance). What he was driving at was for us to realise that to act locally, to try to meet our needs at a local level didn't preclude being linked to bigger systems. He was also trying to make us see that by trying to make sure we could be nourished directly, immediately, as a tree is, is something to aim for. Humans, as monkeys, are always chattering (as I am now) always looking around, always seeking the new, but a tree just stands, having developed highly successful strategies of getting what it needs right here, right now, it can meet all its needs easily.

Permaculture does have something of a Taoist style. The aim is to be rich with less, to live simply through being enmeshed in a web of rich and complex interactions, to do without doing. Remember that although the ideas of permaculture can be applied in an number of different spheres, the system evolved as a gardening method. Anyone who has ever done double digging will know how difficult that process is. The permaculture approach would be to say, well there are times when double digging is needed, but perhaps we can find ways of breaking up the soil, of removing weeds that involve doing less, and maybe if we are lucky we can hit on a system that will give us the yields we need with only minimal intervention and effect. Doing without doing.

Now from the point of view of getting some veggies onto your plate this isn't just an impossible dream. It's probably significant that the notion of permaculture was developed in Australia. The landscape of Australia is quite different from that of north western Europe. Sadly the agriculture of Australia for the most part has been imported lock, stock and barrel with the European settlers who arrived there. So whereas in Britain you can get away (just) with deep ploughing, in Australia which does not have deep glacial soils, you plough and the land literally turns to red dust and blows away. Much of the Australian ecology is based on fire. Trees such as eucalyptus need to burn so that they release the energy held in the canopy and this can help new seeds germinate. In Europe most of the fertility of the land is held in the soil itself and the trick is to watch out for fertility running out of the land with our heavier rainfall.

Bill Mollison and David Holmgren realised that the most productive and sustainable approach to the landscape was to try to work with the native ecology and they experimented with lots of different techniques aimed at creating mutually supportive relationships between the plants they wanted to grow. These techniques included processes that people might be familiar with as companion planting. Let me give you an example:

There is a system of planting often called the Three Sisters in the agricultural systems of some Native American groups in North America. In this method of companion planting three crops are planted close together:

Several maize seeds are planted close together, in the centre of a mound of soil.
When the maize is 6 inches tall, beans and squash are planted around the maize, alternating between beans and squash.
The maize provides a structure for the beans to climb, eliminating the need for poles. The beans provide the nitrogen to the soil that the other plants remove. The squash spreads along the ground,

monopolizing the sunlight to prevent weeds.
The squash also acts as a "living mulch," creating a microclimate to retain moisture in the soil.

So let's look at some of the concepts within permaculture, some of design elements that make it what it is.
One idea is that of Zoning. This means looking at your place, the land we inhabit in terms of a series of areas, often modelled as concentric circles with blurred boundaries.

Zoning is a way of designing to maximise energy efficiency in which activities are put in different zones, depending on frequency of use, maintenance, visits etc.

Generally, activities and structures are placed as follows:

Zone 0: Centre of activities - the house. This is high maintenance, high use and requires considerable investment of time and energy.
Zone 1: Annual plants, herbs, compost, bike store and other high use activities.
Zone 2: Chickens, other animals, orchard, greenhouse.
Zone 3: Water storage, main crops, field shelters.
Zone 4: Forestry, pasture, dams, forage.
Zone 5: Wild zone, where nature is in charge and where we go to learn and harvest only that which is abundant.

Zoning is about using time, energy and resources wisely, which can be as simple as planting your most used herbs nearest to your kitchen, or as complex as planning a community.

This idea of zoning is one that has all kinds of implications. One of the most obvious is that the idealised permaculture farm would generally be a clearing within a forest. This reminds me somewhat of the idea of the clearing in the centre of the Druid internal grove. I worked for a while on a farm in Spain that was run on permaculture principles. One of the interesting things about the farm was that from the opposite side of the valley it was virtually invisible. Only the presence of a few lighter green fruit trees (differing from the surrounding cork oak and pine) betrayed its existence. On some seriously steep sloping land was a tremendously productive series of terraced gardens, and it was self sufficient in 90%

of its food for the seven or so people who lived there at any one time. In part this farm was so productive (even though it was a part of Spain that is very hot for much of the year and with fairly thin soil) because it was embedded so successfully in the wilderness. It benefited from the animals, the shelter, the forage yields of firewood and mushrooms and in many other ways from this wilderness

Permaculture is concerned with the web, the network of life and seeks to maximise the number of positive interactions between elements in a system. The key to doing this is in the design.

One way of using a green house is to use sterile compost that comes from miles away, grow some annual seeds that have been bought from the garden centre and try your best to keep out any nasty insects by keeping the door shut and spraying with pesticides. Obviously in the winter you'll need a fossil fuel driven heater and perhaps a fan in the summer.

Alternatively you could take a few pointers from permaculture:

Consider the relative location of elements.
Each element performs many functions.
Each important function is supported by many elements.
Efficient energy planning: zone, sector and slope.
Using biological resources.
Cycling of energy, nutrients, and resources.
Small-scale intensive systems
Edge effects.

How would the polytunnel look different with the application of some of these ideas?

We'll here's just one way; it might have a pond in it.

Frogs can be introduced into the pond to eat slugs, the water helps humidify and acts as a heat sink to keep the greenhouse at an even temperature. Insects use the pond to drink and can then assist in pollination of plants. The transpiration from plants can be trapped and used to top up the pond. Fish could be grown in the pond for human or high protein animal feed. Fish poo will allow water plants such as Chinese water chestnuts to flourish. The water chestnuts are a relatively exotic plant and therefore may be resistant to local diseases and pests.

By using exotic crops we can broaden our diet, consume less monoculture grain and even end up with a valuable cash crop. The water chestnuts are highly prized for their nutty flavour and their crispness. Eaten raw or cooked they are a gourmet delight. Their nutritional and medicinal properties make them a good commercial crop. The fact that they are easily grown and are a heavy yielding plant is an extra bonus. The activity of animals in the polytunnel will increase the CO_2 levels, help move the air about etc. Obviously the pond should be sited at the lowest point of the polytunnel (perhaps by following the natural slope of the land and the shape would be designed to maximise capture and retention of water. The pond probably needs to be at the far end from the door, the local equivalent of zone 5, the wilderness, so the inhabitants don't get too disturbed by human activity. Because the pond creates an ecotone, an edge between land and water and especially if the system is accelerated by something like using black stone slabs to soak up heat (and provide a path) during the day, the yields of the polytunnel could be really quite something.

Permaculture is not a set of rules; it is a process of design based around principles found in the natural world, of co-operation and mutually beneficial relationships, and translating these principles into actions. But this doesn't mean wading into a system, whether it be an ecology, a community or an allotment, and changing things without spending a lot of time observing.

"Maximum contemplation; minimum action". Permaculture is about thinking before you act. Permaculture inspired action can range from choosing what you eat, how you travel, the type of work you do, and where you live, to working with others to create a community food-growing project. It's about making decisions that relate to all your other decisions; so one area of your life is not working against another. For example, if you are planning a journey, consider other tasks that can be completed on the way to your destination (combining a trip to the leisure centre with buying food on the way home, for example).

It means thinking about your life or project as a whole system - working out the most effective way to do things that involves the least effort and the least damage to others, and looking for ways to make relationships more beneficial.

It is essential to observe your surroundings before making choices. Taking stock at the beginning of a project (whether it be building a house or planting a window box) of the available resources in terms of time, materials, skills, money, opportunities, land etc, and thinking about how these resources can relate to each other is a useful basis for designing a sustainable and effective system. To take the example of a garden - careful observation over the course of a few months can give information about the sunniest spots, the path of a neighbourhood fox, which areas are sheltered from the wind. Such information is not always immediately available, but can ultimately be very important.

"If we want to move on and create sustainability and a more fulfilling quality of life, the best way to do this is to understand the nature of the world and to live harmoniously and creatively with it - to understand that we are a part of the web of life, not separate from it."

But is there more to permaculture? Is it just about getting nicer food, stopping the destruction of wild spaces or of getting better town planning? Well, no, there's a lot more to it than that. There is a vital ethical dimension to permaculture, what we might call the spirituality of permaculture. This is the gardening of zone 00; our selves. Permaculture ethics can be described as being elements of an overall 'life ethic'.

It is important to stress that whilst these are often called the 'permaculture ethics', they are not by any means exclusive to permaculture. Bill Mollison in his research was deliberately looking for the highest common denominator - a set of ethics that were inclusive and broad enough for wide adoption. Permaculture shares these ethics with many other religions, worldviews and belief systems. You can be a Buddhist permaculture designer, or a Hindu, Atheist, Methodist, Communist, Socialist, and possibly even a capitalist....

The ethics can be likened to a compass, guiding us towards a world in which we care for ourselves, others and the earth that sustains us. We're not there yet, but with a clear sense of direction, we can work steadily towards a more sustainable human culture with each of our actions. These ethics are generally divided into three main categories:

Earth Care
Permaculture as a design system is based on natural systems. It is about

working with nature, not against it - not using natural resources unnecessarily or at a rate at which they cannot be replaced. Conservation of biodiversity, clean air and water, restoration and conservation of forests, habitats and soils, recycling and pollution reduction, conservation of energy and natural resources, appropriate technology. It also means using outputs from one system as inputs for another (vegetable peelings as compost, for example), and so minimising wastage.

People Care

People care is about looking after us as people, not just the world we live in. It works on both an individual and a community level. Self-reliance, co-operation and support of each other should be encouraged. Health and well-being, nourishment with good food, lifelong learning, right livelihood and meaningful work, community belonging, open communication, plus trust and respect. People care is also about our legacy to future generations.

Fair Shares

The fair shares part of the permaculture ethic brings earth care and people care together. We only have one earth, and we have to share it - with each other, with other living things, and with future generations. This means limiting our consumption, especially of natural resources, and working for everyone to have access to the fundamental needs of life - clean water, clean air, food, shelter, meaningful employment, and social contact. Fair share is all about co-operation, networking and sharing, distribution of resources and wealth, reduction of consumerism, rethinking current notions of growth, progress and development, making a contribution.

Permaculture does not provide prescriptive solutions to the problems facing the world - nobody is going to demand that you put a herb spiral in the bottom left corner of your garden, or wear only hand knitted recycled non-bleached organic fair trade clothes. It is about allowing you the freedom to observe your surroundings, and make decisions that will work for you, in your situation, using the resources you have. And it's not just about a Romantic return to wild nature. For the challenges that are all around us in the world cannot be met successfully, unless we try to make intelligent human judgements that are both holistic and just. When we look at ecological issues, at green politics, it's easy to get focused on specific problems that face us; climate change, genetically manipulated crops, epidemic levels of autoimmune disease and more. But we can't tackle any one of these issues without thinking ecologically, realising that increased fossil fuel use leads to climate change, that in the drive to produce more food faster we are willing to make short term gains through the use of GM crops. That pesticide contamination from non-organic food leads to asthma epidemics and so on and so forth. To look at these issues we need to look ecologically, holistically and we need to put the notion of justice firmly in the picture. Because unless we try to create a world that is just, a world that is fair, we'll just end up shifting the problems round and round rather than solving any of them: just as surely as warfare leads to famine, famine to disease and disease to refugees and the destruction of social, economic and environmental systems.

So I'm sure you can already see there are lots of features that are common to both Druidry and permaculture.

Permaculture is about creating sustainable human habitats by following nature's patterns. It uses the diversity, stability and resilience of natural ecosystems to provide a framework and guidance for people to develop their own sustainable solutions to the problems facing their world, on a local, national or global scale. It is based on the philosophy of co-operation with nature and caring for the earth and its people. We can see exactly the same processes in Druidry where we learn to understand ourselves by looking for teachings from animals, trees and other beings.

In his article on Druidry and Politics Philip Carr-Gomm writes about his predecessor Ross Nichols "…championing monetary reform, pacifism and socialism…(he) believed passionately in the need for us to return to a closer relationship with Nature…to retreat often to the countryside, to living on the land in as simple a way as possible…practising Druidry - a spirituality which has as its aim this return to a communion with the natural world."

Permaculture seeks to foster the skills, confidence and imagination to enable people to become self-reliant, and to seek creative solutions to problems on a global or local scale, in the same way that Druidry seeks to increase our creativity and our ability to express that creativity. It also places our own development in the context of the wider community. Even if you're a solitary Druid the emphasis on justice, on being ethical, in the Druid's prayer, calls on us to 'walk our talk', to take our spiritual practice out into the world of human morality. "...And in Knowledge, the Knowledge of Justice"

And it is in terms of the ideas of justice, of walking the talk, that Druidry and permaculture really mesh together.

From some of the classical sources I've checked it does seem that the ancient Druids were arbiters in disputes and advisers to decision makers. And what we can be certain of is that the modern Druid tradition as expressed in the Druids prayer, places great emphasis on our ability to judge and be just.

Druidry, as a pagan spiritual path is about seeing the self as part of the whole and it is specifically about learning how, given that perspective, to act ethically.

Now it goes without saying that the world would be much better if Druids ran it. Obviously we don't necessarily want a world run by Wiccans (too much drunkenness) or, Gods forbid chaos magicians (we'd be up to our eyeballs in weird sexual practices and even weirder drugs!). But us Druids, well I reckon we could do a pretty good job.

So although what permaculture practice is most explicitly about is garden design, at its heart is the notion of care, of attempting to nurture the people and other systems on the planet in order to create 'fair share' and an equitable and just society. This practice is, for me, the essence of Druidry.

Phil Carr-Gomm says that the word justice is a key concept in his article on Druidry and Politics:

> "Druidry has always been concerned with Justice. In the old days Druids were judges and law-makers. And if we expand the concept to include Social Justice and Economic Justice we can start to see what the term implies... Our world is so full of social and economic injustices of every kind, that it seems to me that a spirituality where Justice is a key concept, and where its early practitioners were actually responsible for administering justice,

can quite legitimately begin to engage the big question of 'How can we build a more just world?" And this big question immediately raises another one: 'What would our world look like if there was more justice?' How would we live?' These questions move us towards the exciting and creative area of envisioning the future and of trying to create a better way of living together ,'of community.'"

So to live what has been described as an 'ecological lifestyle' is identical with the attempt to be a just man or woman. To aim to nurture a world, to show care for the world in order to create a world based on the vision of 'us' is what I think Phillip means when he says community.

In practice, this does not mean each person growing enough food to feed themselves in their back garden; it means that as many as possible of the inputs for a community (food, skills etc) come from within that community. While the individual has a part to play, in most places it is not realistic for an individual household to provide for all of their own needs in terms of food, clothing, work etc, and the emphasis is more on self-reliance and increased sufficiency within the community, rather than individual self-sufficiency.

Modern Druidry, our style of Druidry, is very much part of this process that is engaged in developing a spirituality that exists in community, making that connection between self and nature, living simply, showing care for the earth, and doing this always with the idea of fairshare, the 'knowledge of justice' in mind.

Phillip goes on to say how Ross:

"...didn't want all this just for himself. He had a political and social conscience that meant his idealism was not unrealistic, selfish or elitist. He wanted everyone to benefit from the ideals he believed in hence his commitment to socialism and the Social Credit movement, which attempted to completely re-vision the way we deal with money. In other words his idealism was practical, it was grounded in his actions and behaviour as well as in his philosophy and in his heart."

And I guess if there is a central message from this talk it echoes the practice of Ross Nichols. That message emerges in the beliefs of permaculturists, the Druids and many others: that care for the earth and concern for social justice must go hand in hand. We cannot successfully love the earth unless we love each other and that love of each other is supported by the ability to share.

Now one of the things I really like about permaculture is its real practicality. So what I'd like to do now is two things. The first is to run through some permaculture tips I've picked up. Of course I'm sure you all have some wonderful ideas, questions and observations about these points so what I've done is put a large sheet of paper at the back of the hall and some pens. Please, over the course of the day, share you ideas and insights by writing on these sheets - you might be able to plant a seed of an idea that could grown into something quite extraordinary.

So, some practical tips that I thought of when I was asked to deliver this talk. What is the realpolitik?

1. Local production. There is a lot to be said for learning actual gardening, even if that's limited to sprouting some cress on the windowsill. In part, gardening is about healing the industrial split that is particularly deep in British culture. In 1800 20% of people in this country lived in cities and the rest in the country. By1900 80% of the population lived in urban environments. We literally got cut off from our roots, from the production of food and shelter. Growing produce, becoming producers, a few salad vegetables, fruit, foraging for wild food, making compost and taking it to the local allotment, guerrilla gardening; all these processes help move us back from the perspective of passive consumer to active producer.

2. We can spend money locally. Money is like water and just as good management of land looks at how best to retain, recycle and reuse water in the landscape, we need to do the same for money. To use the jargon of permaculture we need 'maximum possible uses between source and sink'. This means making sure that when money comes into our communities it passes around as much as possible before it leaves. Shopping locally, avoiding spending our money in chain stores and looking at where we invest. If we have capital this means placing money in local projects or looking to local credit unions, ethical investment and

banks. (Triodos bank, the Ecology building society have good records.)

3. When centralised authority is active look at strategies for taking power back. This happened recently in my part of the world where, as a result of edicts from central government, the county council massively cut the funding to adult and community learning. The result, many tutors simply opened their own classes and a few are starting to band together to offer mutual support etc.

4. Buy fair-trade when we need to consume something from far away. And, obviously, cutting our consumption. Watch out for empty 'green consumerism'. For example I get a bit nervous about the current vogue for carbon balancing. Some of seems to me a bit like the Church selling 'indulgencies'. That is, offering to pray for your soul in return for you parting with money. Whilst carbon balancing is useful it only works as part of a whole package, including limiting and reducing consumption. Some ways to reduce our consumption are really simple. For example I remember visiting Rae Beth when she lived in a housing estate on the outskirts of Bath. She and her partner used an earth fridge. As vegetarians they didn't need to keep meat fresh so a stone lined hole in the suburban garden was fine for keeping cheese and soya milk cool. Leave the bathwater in the bath and use it to flush the toilet. There are so many ways to cut consumption and as the supermarkets themselves will remind us, 'every little helps'.

5. Start here and now. You don't have to wait to develop a 'permaculture lifestyle' none of these things is dependent on having an acre of land in the countryside, a renovated barn in Spain, or anything else. You don't need to own your own home or live in a rural situation to make a significant difference.

6. Give away excess. Very simple this one. If you have too much of a resource consider giving away what you can't immediately use.

7. Find our current niches. My partner and I have little time for gardening with a young family. We keep a few chickens and grow some fruit and salad greens but our great skill is in organisation. So what we do to support local production is organise a seed swap in our area. This means that local gardeners get together to swap rare and heritage varieties of

163

seeds. In this way we use our specialist skills to support small holdings and especially organic gardeners in the region.

8. Come together, campaign and engage with decision making. Vote, write to the papers, and talk to colleagues, family and friends.

9. Be conscious of the need to heal the divides between different parts of our global community and recognise that healing takes time and support.

10. Don't adopt dogma. Or as I think it was the Discordians put it, 'death to fanatics!' Permaculture does not necessarily mean only gardening organically. There are circumstances where you might need to use chemical pesticide, for instance. It's about negotiation, process and not being resolutely wedded to immovable ideology.

11. Avoid debt. Remember that debt is often an important part of capitalist systems running hot, increasing

consumption, encouraging production where wages and conditions of production get worse and worse. Find ways of trading that don't rely on money. Try LETS systems, swapping, bartering.

12. Be aware of the lifecycle of any resource, any object that comes into your hands. Remember that the planet is round and that we can't really throw anything away!

13. Seek to see resources shared fairly. Land is the first wealth and the type of wealth we can't manufacture more of. Access to land, for recreation, foraging, growing and dwelling is a key area to get involved with, whether you're helping maintain footpaths or squatting empty buildings.

14. Create diversity, the chaotically rich cottage garden rather than the prairie monoculture. Get two part time jobs rather than just one full time one. Get your resources from a range of places. Be individual and look to maintain local distinctiveness.

15. Continue and develop your spiritual practice. Nourish the self like a tree, through beauty, ecstasy and love. Change from competition to co-operation and away from selfishness to compassion and care.

And finally

The problem from a permaculture perspective has been a lack of design. Agriculture, from its invention 10,000 years ago onwards, has generally involved clearing the wilderness and establishing a cycle of digging, ploughing, then seeding with a few useful species, primarily grasses, then harvesting the crop to feed humans and livestock - and the cycle begins again year on year until the land is exhausted. In some places (such as the rich glacial soils of the British Isles), this process works reasonably successfully. In other landscapes, the fertility of the soil declines until even huge doses of imported fertiliser are not enough and the soil structure begins to collapse.

The solution from a permaculture perspective is to introduce design into agriculture in order to create permanent high-yielding agricultural ecosystems, so that humans can thrive on as little land as possible, thus leaving as much land as possible as wilderness, if necessary helping the wilderness re-establish itself.

In order to implement this global vision, we need local solutions, because every place on earth is different in local climate, land form, soils, and the combinations of species which will thrive. Not only does the land and its potential vary from place to place, but so do the people vary in their needs and preferences and their capacities. Every place and community requires its own particular design. Hence at the local level, permaculture designers often refer to permaculture as being about designing for 'permanent culture'.

Permaculture means different things to different people. One person may interpret it in a practical sense in terms of growing food, perhaps, while another will focus on a more spiritual side. This diversity is important; it helps to keep a sense of balance, and encourages people to share their resources and knowledge with others. Working together is the key - it takes a lot of strain off the individual. It is also important to be well informed and if you can help others, spread your knowledge in return.

So I'd like to finish by offering a little resource that I use. When faced with the horror, the destruction, the stupidity of our actions as a species I often think about the problem using the Star Trek metaphor. Remember all those episodes where the wise ancient alien species tolerate us because we are just a young culture? As a whole species we're only just at the beginning of our process for developing a really holistic view of our planet and ourselves. We're young and a bit daft. We've only been doing agriculture for a few thousand years and living in big groups for even less. We've only just created industrial technologies for mass production and it's not been five minutes since we've created global systems for sharing knowledge. Sure we shouldn't make light of the injustices and pain that we inflict on our own and other species, but neither should we write us off as inherently evil. We're only just beginning to realise that our own happiness is dependent upon the actions of others. Once we really understand this we can then realize that we secure our own happiness by concerning ourselves with the happiness of others. By making others happy, we often also serve ourselves. By making others unhappy, we often bring unhappiness to ourselves.

Through the kind of ethical actions that permaculture embodies we come to a real lived-in understanding of the relatedness of all things. As we might say in the vocabulary of Druidry; through the love of justice we discover the love of all existences.

Index

O

octarine 96
Odin 99
Old Religion 89
One Star In Sight 43, 50
Opium 73
Ori 52, 57, 61, 64, 65, 88
Orisha 55, 90
Orpheus, Rodney 43
Osiris 64

P

pagan 4, 53, 82, 125, 134, 142, 146, 147, 157
Paganism 103, 126, 134, 141
Pan 14, 43, 44
parapsychological 5, 103
parapsychology 106
Parvati 66
pathworking 6, 76, 90, 105
pentagram 10, 13, 14, 15, 31, 32, 135, 136
Perry, Lee 'Scratch' 55
peyote 76, 145
Pharmakon 29, 48, 77, 103, 121
Pilkington, Mark 117
piñata 53, 60
Pomba Gira 34, 88, 89, 90, 91, 92, 93, 94, 95
prana 113
Pratchett, Terry 120
pregnancy 55, 63
Psilocybin. See See mushrooms
Psybermagick 66
psychedelic 17, 19, 20, 21, 24, 75, 76, 98, 107, 115, 143, 146
psychedelics 18, 21, 99, 106, 110, 121, 122
psychogeography 38, 97, 98, 101
psychotopography 28
puja 67

Q

Qabalah 3, 14, 27, 28, 43, 72, 73, 74, 76, 105, 106, 142
Qabalistic 6, 65
quantum physics 5, 47, 106

R

Ra-Hoor-Khuit 30, 33, 35, 65
Regardie, Israel 104
Reichenbach, Baron von 104

S

Sacks, Oliver 110
salvia divinorum 146
Satan 14, 15
sex 11, 22, 23, 27, 28, 29, 85, 106
sexual 25, 27, 126, 142, 157
shaman 23, 24, 25, 26, 27, 28, 29, 66, 76, 101, 130, 141, 143, 145
shamanic 17, 23, 25, 26, 28, 75, 76, 100, 123, 143
shamanism 6, 23, 27, 75, 85, 131, 143
Shulgin, Alexander 77, 107, 122
siddhi 41, 70
sigil 95, 135
sigilisation 70, 100
Skinner, B.F. 107
socialism 156, 158
soil 36, 150, 152, 162
Spain 151, 160
Spare, Austin Osman 23, 29, 52, 70, 71
spirit 18, 20, 22, 23, 27, 36, 74, 78, 81, 83, 86, 92, 97, 99, 100, 114, 115, 117, 118, 122
St Paul 12
Star Trek 119, 163
Starhawk 7, 82, 83, 87
Strange Attractor 117
Sufi 30

Photography courtesy of Peter Gray, with apologies to Orlando

Mandrake

'Books you don't see everyday'

Bright From the Well by Dave Lee
978-1869928-841, £10.99

'Bright From the Well' consists of five stories plus five essays and a rune-poem. The stories revolve around themes from Norse myth - the marriage of Frey and Gerd, the story of how Gullveig-Heidh reveals her powers to the gods, a modern take on the social-origins myth Rig's Tale, Loki attending a pagan pub moot and the Ragnarok seen through the eyes of an ancient shaman.

The essays include examination of the Norse creation or origins story, of the magician in or against the world and a chaoist's magical experiences looked at from the standpoint of Northern magic.'

'Dave Lee coaches breathwork, writes fiction and non-fiction, blends incenses and oils, creates music and collages'

The Apophenion: A Chaos Magic Paradigm by Peter J Carroll.
978-1869928-421, £10.99

My final Magnum Opus if its ideas remain unfalsified within my lifetime, otherwise its back to the drawing board. Yet I've tried to keep it as short and simple as possible, it consists of eight fairly brief and terse chapters and five appendices.

It attacks most of the great questions of being, free will, consciousness, meaning, the nature of mind, and humanity's place in the cosmos, from a magical perspective. Some of the conclusions seem to challenge many of the deeply held assumptions that our culture has taught us, so brace yourself for the paradigm crash and look for the jewels revealed in the wreckage.

This book contains something to offend everyone; enough science to upset the magicians, enough magic to upset the scientists, and enough blasphemy to upset most trancendentalists.

"The most original, and probably the most important, writer on Magick since Aleister Crowley."

-Robert Anton Wilson, author of the *Cosmic Trigger* trilogy.

Other Mandrake Titles:
Fries/*Cauldron of the Gods: a manual of Celtic Magick.*
552pp, royal octavo, 9781869928612 £24.99$40 paper

Fries/*Seidways Shaking, Swaying and Serpent Mysteries.* 350pp
9781869928360 £15/$25
Still the definitive and much sought after study of magical trance and possession techniques.

Fries/*Helrunar - a manual of rune magick.* 454pp 9781968828902 pbk,
£19.99/$40 Over 130 illustrations. new enlarged and improved edition
'*...eminently practical and certainly breaks new ground.'* - Ronald Hutton

Fries/*Visual Magick: a manual of freestyle shamanism.* 196pp
9781869928575 £10.99/$20. '*A practical modern grimoire.'* The Cauldron

Wilson *I, Crowley - Last Confession of the Beast 666 - Almost*
£9.99/$20 250 pages ISBN 9781869928544, second edition
'*Brilliant . . . the Great Beast explaining himself in lapel-grabbing prose.'*
Simon Callow

Order direct from

Mandrake of Oxford
PO Box 250, Oxford, OX1 1AP (UK)
Phone: 01865 243671
(for credit card sales)
Prices include economy postage
Visit our web site
online at - www.mandrake.uk.net

Lightning Source UK Ltd.
Milton Keynes UK
UKOW031438060312

188444UK00001B/15/P

9 781869 928469